# THE CHRISTIAN'S HERITAGE

George Hall
James Naismith

Christian Missions in Many Lands Inc.
Post Office Box 13
Spring Lake, New Jersey 07762

*Printed in Canada*

# THE CHRISTIAN'S HERITAGE

Two outstanding Bible teachers ministered the Word at a Conference for Believers in 1995 at Greenwood Hills Fayetteville, Pennsylvania. The subject, The Christian's Heritage, was deemed of great importance and the oral ministry was well received and much appreciated.

The conveners, Christian Missions in Many Lands, felt that this material would have much wider impact in book form. The recorded messages have been altered, where appropriate, for a written presentation by brethren George Hall and James Naismith. Typeset by Gertrud Harlow, it is now published in this format.

From the chapter headings we can see that the authors take us from the origins of the Brethren movement in the first chapter to the present trends and dangers in the last. In the intervening chapters they portray the beauty and simplicity of church principles recorded for our learning in the New Testament.

George Hall was a school teacher for many years in Northern Ireland, but now gives himself fully to the Lord's work. He is secretary of "Harvest Fields", a bi-monthly magazine of the work of missionaries associated with the assemblies in Northern Ireland, laboring in many fields. Mr. Hall is well-known as a conference speaker on both sides of the Atlantic.

Dr. James Naismith, born in India of missionary parents, received his medical education and degree at the university of Glasgow. He served in his profession for many years in Scotland and Canada, now living in Toronto. He is in constant demand as a conference speaker in Canada and United States, also India. Two of his books were earlier published by Everyday Publications.

This present volume has great potential for all who love the Lord and seek to obey His Word.

## George Hall

# 1. Our Heritage:
## Where did we come from?

Before embarking upon a consideration of this topic, let us briefly consider the words of Deuteronomy 31:9-13.

*9   And Moses wrote this law, and delivered it unto the priests the sons of Levi, which bare the ark of the covenant of the Lord, and unto all the elders of Israel.*
*10   And Moses commanded them, saying, At the end of every seven years, in the solemnity of the year of release, in the feast of tabernacles,*
*11   When all Israel is come to appear before the Lord thy God in the place which he shall choose, thou shalt read this law before all Israel in their hearing.*
*12   Gather the people together, men, and women, and children, and thy stranger that is within thy gates, that they may hear, and that they may learn, and fear the Lord your God, and observe to do all the words of this law:*
*13   And that their children, which have not known any thing, may hear, and learn to fear the Lord your God, as long as ye live in the land whither ye go over Jordan to possess it.*

It is clear from this passage that once every seven years there was to be held what may be called a very special history lesson, for all the people of Israel. Coinciding with the celebration of the Feast of Tabernacles they were to receive instruction in the Law of the Lord. They were to "hear" and "learn" and then "fear the Lord and observe to do all the words of this law". The purpose of this special recalling of the past was that little children, who heretofore had not received instruction in these matters might become thoroughly acquainted with them, and thus develop an appreciation of their heritage. This seven-year cycle of teaching would systematize and consolidate all the on-going instruction which was enjoined in other Scriptures. (See e.g., Deut. 6:4-9)

It is appropriate that we, too, should reflect from time to time upon the spiritual heritage which we enjoy through our links with 'Brethren Assemblies'; as they are commonly known. It is not our wish to use Biblical terms, such as 'brethren', 'saints' and 'believers' in a sectarian or divisive sense. We recognize that every person who is truly 'born again' has entitlement to these names, yet the reality of today's situation is that we are identified with a movement, the origins of which lie in the early part of the nineteenth century. It is our intention to explore how these assemblies, which I trust we love and support to the utter limit of our capabilities, came into being. As we do so, it is to be hoped that we can sincerely share the sentiments of the writer of Psalm 16 who said, "The lines are fallen to me in pleasant places; yea, I have a goodly heritage."

With reference to the history of the movement, there are two extreme positions which we ought to avoid. On the one hand, there are those who adopt the attitude that what happened one hundred and seventy years ago has no relevance to present-day conditions. We are concerned, they will contend, with serving our own generation, as David was (Acts 13:36) What occurred in 'the early days' has no significance. While this point of view may be held with great sincerity, we must also remember that each of us is, to some degree, the product of his past which, like a mold, shapes us. Past events do have an influence upon us and undoubtedly have lessons to teach us. We cannot totally dismiss the past, as though it did not exist!

The other extreme position is to become so completely anchored to the past as though we are set in concrete, and no change is possible. Those who adopt this attitude will contend that everything must go on in just the same way as it was done a hundred years ago.

The wise course must surely lie between these two extremes. We must take cognizance of the past, and benefit from its legacy, yet also recognize that we are living in a world where the speed of change has reached an unprecedented level. We believe that in the Word of God there are age-enduring principles, which were freshly discovered by 'the early Brethren' in the 1820's. They recovered them from layers of ceremonialism, ritualism and formalism under which these precious truths had become buried for many centuries. Our desire is to practise these principles, not in a sectarian way, but in a warm-hearted manner which will prove to be spiritually attractive to true believers everywhere.

The story begins, to a very large extent, in the British Isles, and even more specifically, in Ireland, about the beginning of the nineteenth century. It was a time 'of very considerable upheaval both politically and religiously. The French Revolution, in the last years of the eighteenth century, had been followed by the Napoleonic Wars, culminating in the Battle of Waterloo in 1815. Throughout Britain the Industrial Revolution was taking place, with the resultant rapid growth of towns and factories and a marked shift of population from rural settings.

On the religious front, there had been the movement headed by the Wesley brothers, resulting in the birth of Methodism. Many missionary societies had come into being. William Carey had sailed for India in 1792, and with his going, there had been the formation of the Baptist Missionary Society. This was followed shortly by the Church Missionary Society and the London Missionary Society. The British and Foreign Bible Society was established in 1804.

It was against this background of political, social and religious change that a spiritual awakening took place. The very deadness of the Established Church — the Church of England — contributed in no small measure to what was about to happen. Added to this was the extreme sectarianism of many of the 'Dissenting Churches' (i.e., those which had broken away from the Church of England). Many true believers were tightly locked into church systems which frowned severely upon fellowship with fellow-believers who were associated with other denominations. Great emphasis was laid upon what was known as 'special membership'. By this was meant that a believer should adhere to a particular church, and have no association with Christians outside that body. Dr. Edward Cronin, to whom we shall refer later, suffered greatly under this legalistic, sectarian procedure.

From this kind of ethos emerged small groups of believers who met in great simplicity and without any central controlling body. They desired to honour only the name of the Lord Jesus, and they claimed His promise, "Where two or three are gathered together in my name, there am I in the midst of them." (Matt. 18:20)

It should be borne in mind that such a movement was not really a new thing. In a sense, it followed a truly 'apostolic succession'. E. H. Broadbent, who was a missionary in Europe at the beginning of the twentieth century, has shown in his book, 'The Pilgrim Church,' that there have always been companies of God's people who met, in simplicity, according to what they found written in the Word. When we speak about the birth of "Brethrenism," therefore, we are not referring to some previously unheard-of teachings. Rather, we are dealing with a recovery, or rebirth, of New Testament truths which had been practised, albeit in a very minor key, down through all the centuries from apostolic times.

It should also be pointed out that this recovery was not the brain-child of any one man. We cannot point today to one specific individual and say, "There is the person who started 'Brethren Assemblies'." Most religious bodies do honour the men and women who are at the foundation of their particular movement. For example, the Methodists point back to John and Charles Wesley, and the Quakers (Society of Friends) revere George Fox as their founder. But today we do not regard any man as the originator of that with which we are identified. It is infinitely more fitting that all the honour goes to our Lord Jesus Christ, and that He be absolutely central in our individual and corporate witness.

## *WHERE DID WE COME FROM?*

The 'early Brethren' as we may speak of them, did not set out to form another denomination. Having seen the errors of denominationalism, it was certainly not their intention to add to the confusion which was already existing. They grasped with freshness and enthusiasm the truth of the oneness of the body of Christ, (Eph.1:22,23, Col.1:18) and in seeking to give expression to this truth, they were binding believers together, rather than breaking them apart. We cannot fairly be accused of forming a new denomination if we revert to what was taught and practised by the apostles in the beginning of the Church era, without, recourse to man-made rules but solely following the Word of God.

The circumstances surrounding the inception of the movement are such that one is led to the conclusion that the Spirit of God was working amongst His people. Spontaneously, in different locations and without consultation with one another, believers began to meet together in a very simple and unstructured fashion to study the Scriptures, to praise God and to celebrate together the Lord's Supper. It was essentially a 'Back to the Bible' movement!

Let us come now more definitively to the characters and events of 'the early days.'

The name of Dr. Edward Cronin has already been mentioned. He was born in Cork, Ireland, in 1801, the child of a Roman Catholic father and a Protestant mother. He came as a medical student to Dublin about 1825. By this time, he was a true believer in the Lord Jesus and was accepted to the Lord's table, as a visitor in Dublin, but when he became a settled resident this privilege was refused him. He was informed that he could no longer be admitted to 'Communion' without 'special membership'. This meant that he would have to join one particular church and dissociate himself from all others. Cronin had no objection to joining a church, but the idea of separating himself from other believers grieved him deeply. "I loved them all," he wrote, and he found it difficult to take a step which would cut him off from fellowship with other Christians.

11

Cronin persisted in frequenting a variety of Dublin churches, until a certain Rev. W. Cooper of York St. Independent Church denounced him from the pulpit one Sunday morning as 'a wicked person'! It was a severe blow to a young man seeking Christian fellowship! Concerning these happenings, Cronin wrote, "This affected me to such an extent that it was a season of deep exercise of heart, and separation from many that I loved in the Lord; and to avoid the appearance of evil I spent many a Lord's Day morning under a hay-stack or a tree, during the time of their services. My name having been publicly denounced from the pulpit, one of the deacons, Edward Wilson, was constrained to protest against this step, which led ultimately to his leaving also. Thus separated, we two met for breaking of bread and prayer in one of his rooms, until his departure for England."

This was 1825, and may be viewed as the first meeting on the ground afterwards taken by 'Brethren'. Before long, others joined them.

About this time, another development was taking place. The names associated with this part of the story are Anthony Norris Groves, John Nelson Darby, John Gifford Bellett and John Parnell, who afterwards became Lord Congleton.

Groves had been born in England in 1795. He was converted at Exeter, and on qualifying as a dentist, established a lucrative practice, but within a short time relinquished it with a view of becoming a missionary. When he presented himself to a missionary society, he was informed that without ecclesiastical ordination he would not be permitted to 'administer the sacraments'. Being convinced that the Lord was calling him to missionary service, Groves came to Dublin to study theology at Trinity College with a view to being 'ordained for the ministry'.

While he was engaged in his studies, he met a fellow student, J.G. Bellett. Together they attended Bible-readings at the beautiful mansion of Lady Powerscourt, in Co. Wicklow, south of Dublin. Bellett was a man of fine intellect, but also a deeply spiritual man, as is clearly evidenced by his writings.

Perhaps his best known books are 'The Son of God' and 'The Moral Glories of the Lord Jesus'.

As Groves and Bellett studied the Scriptures together, there came to them a wonderful understanding which to them was exciting in its newness. It was expressed thus by Bellett: "Groves has just been telling me that it appeared to him from the Scripture that believers meeting together, as disciples of Christ, were free to break bread together as their Lord had admonished them, and that, in as far as the practice of the apostles could be a guide, every Lord's Day should be set apart for thus remembering the Lord's death and obeying His parting command."

This 'discovery' was followed by others. Of great importance was the conviction that grew in Groves' mind that human ordination was completely unnecessary! Here is what he had to say about it: "One day the thought was brought to my mind that ordination of any kind to preach the Gospel is no requirement of Scripture. To me it was the removal of a mountain. From that moment I have myself never had a doubt of my liberty in Christ to minister the Word."

Groves shared his thoughts with others, with the result that very soon a little meeting for the Breaking of Bread was commenced. J.G. Bellett has left on record his memories of these remarkable days: "Walking one day with Groves, as we were passing down Lower Pembroke Street, he said to me, 'This I doubt not is the mind of God concerning us — we should come together in all simplicity as disciples, not waiting on any pulpit or ministry, but trusting that the Lord would edify us together by ministering as He pleased and saw good from the midst of ourselves.' At the moment he spoke these words I was assured my soul had got the right idea, and that moment I remember as if it were but yesterday, and could point you out the place. It was the birthday of my mind, may I so speak, as a brother."

Another outstanding man in these 'early days' was John Nelson Darby. Born in 1800, he was a man of great ability, a classical scholar, a gold medallist of Trinity College and an accomplished linguist. He studied law and was called to the Irish Chancery Bar but abandoned that calling on the grounds of conscience. Instead, he became a clergyman in the Church of Ireland, and was appointed to the parish of Calary, in Co. Wicklow. He, too, attended the Bible studies at nearby Powerscourt; with his incisive mind and great intellectual gifts, he became one of the forces of that distinguished company.

About 1830, the two groups — that of Cronin and that of Groves, Bellett and Darby — came together, forming one meeting. A private house was no longer sufficiently large for their requirements, so they rented an auction room in Aungier Street, Dublin. Cronin has left this account of these developments: "We soon began to feel, as humbler brethren were added to us, that the house in Fitzwilliam Square was unsuited. This led us to take a large auction room in Aungier Street for use on the Sundays, and oh! the blessed seasons with my soul, with John Parnell, William Stokes and others, while moving the furniture aside and laying the simple table with its bread and wine on Saturday evenings, seasons of joy never to be forgotten, for surely we had the Master's smile and sanction, in the beginning of such a movement as this was."

It is evident that these men were acting out of deep conviction, the basis of which was the Word of God. It is true to say that they were men of great natural ability and of high educational standards, but all these assets had been made subservient to the Word of God, and to the Lordship of Christ. H.A. Ironside, in his book 'A Historical Sketch of the Brethren Movement' has summed up their main convictions in this way:

1. The Lord's Supper is not the badge or the exclusive possession of one sect or party.

2. No ordained clergyman is needed to preside over the celebration of the Lord's Supper.

3. The presence of the Lord is guaranteed to any two or three gathered together in the name of Jesus, whether for prayer, worship, or to take the feast of love.

4. Scripture contains no evidence of a clerical system in

the early church; indeed, the Word teaches the priesthood of all true believers.

Dublin was not the only place where such convictions were being formed. In Plymouth, England, two outstanding men were Benjamin Wills Newton, a Scholar and Fellow of Oxford University, and Captain Percy Francis Hall. The latter had been a commander in the Royal Navy, but had resigned his commission for conscience sake. Arising out of the association of these two, a Breaking of Bread was established. It developed very rapidly, and at one stage there were 1,200 believers gathering each Lord's Day in a simple fashion. They had a very vigorous Gospel witness in the Plymouth area, and as they went to surrounding towns and villages to evangelize, people asked, "Who are these people? Where do they come from?" The simple reply was, "They come from Plymouth and they call themselves 'Brethren'. Thus the name 'Plymouth Brethren' was coined, and it remains quite commonly used to this present time.

Another center was Bristol, with which is linked the name of George Müller. Born in Germany in 1806 he led a particularly sinful life, until his conversion to Christ resulted in a complete about-turn, and he became a man of most remarkable devotion and faith. He is especially remembered for his work in the Ashley Downs Orphanage where he took care, through the years, of more than 10,000 orphans. The entire operation was a 'work of faith', for Müller never asked for one penny for all that massive undertaking. His story is, indeed, a wonderful testimony to faith in God.

During his years at Bristol, Müller was closely associated with Henry Craik, a highly educated Scot, who came to Exeter to become tutor to the family of A.N. Groves. After a period of time, Craik moved to Bristol where his powerful exposition of Scripture and his careful shepherding of the Flock were deeply appreciated by many.

The expansion of the movement was rapid and far-reaching. H.A. Ironside comments, "In a number of instances, as the teaching became known, clergymen and their entire congregations accepted the teachings of 'Brethren' with deep exercise, and bodily separated themselves from existing systems." The 'Popular Encyclopaedia' in its article on 'Plymouth Brethren' states: "It seemed at first to be a movement large enough to threaten the whole organisation of the Christian Church."

J.N. Darby traveled extensively on the continent of Europe especially in France and Switzerland. Later, he ministered the Word in Canada, U.S.A., West Indies and New Zealand. For over fifty years he strenuously engaged in the exposition of Scripture, and is remembered as preacher, writer, translator of the Bible and hymn-writer.

A.N. Groves endured great hardship and personal sacrifice in carrying the Gospel to Bagdad, and later to India. Under God, he laid the foundation of much of the missionary endeavour which has characterised 'Brethren Assemblies' in subsequent years.

Many other names might be mentioned, but time and space forbid. Enough has been recorded to indicate that this was not a humanly-engineered movement, controlled by a central body. It is much more in accordance with the facts to say that the Spirit of God was drawing the people of God back to a simple adherence to the principles of the Word of God. With freshness and vitality these principles were accepted in many parts of the world, and it was demonstrated that they were as workable in the nineteenth century as they were in the first!

What were the main tenets of these 'early Brethren'? Let us attempt to summarise them thus:

*1. The unity in Christ of all believers.*

In their thinking and teaching, they aimed at drawing a circle, so to speak, which would include all the children of God, and exclude none. Cronin has written, "'Special membership', as it was called among Dissenters, was the primary and most offensive condition of things to our minds." Darby wrote, "No meeting which is not framed to embrace all the children of God in the full basis of the kingdom of the Son can find the fullness of blessing." Müller's words underscore the point, "We ought to receive all whom Christ has received, irrespective of the measure of grace or knowledge which they have attained unto."

What a delightful and Biblical concept this is! It needs to be handled very sensitively by men of deep spirituality. The sad fact is that even in these 'early days' of which we have been thinking, dissensions and divisions arose with a blighting effect upon the tender plant which was emerging from the arid deadness of the prevailing ecclesiastical scene.

*2. They believed in the authority and the total reliability of the Word of God.*

They were 'men of the Book'; their minds were saturated with the words of Holy Scripture. Of J.N. Darby it is said that he 'lived in the Bible' and he recommended `thinking in Scripture'. Dr. Thomas Neatby, who wrote a history of the 'Brethren' in 1901, said, "The minds of the 'Brethren' were saturated with the words of Scripture; they talked of them when they sat in their homes and when they walked by the way, when they lay down and when they rose up. Conversational Bible Readings were their principal recreation, and, in fact, an invitation to tea might almost be taken to imply an invitation to social Bible study." In this regard, they have left us a fine heritage. Our individual and corporate testimony is weakened in direct proportion to our neglect of Holy Scripture.

*3. The importance of the Lord's Supper, on a weekly basis.*

*4. The priesthood of all believers.*

The commonly accepted distinction between "clergy" and "laity" was rejected, as being without scriptural authority.

*5. The imminent Second Coming of the Lord Jesus.*

Amongst the 'early Brethren' there was a tremendous upsurge of interest in prophetic studies.

*6. The propagation of the Gospel.*

These years were marked by widespread and fruitful evangelism. It has been said that J.N. Darby seldom preached the

Gospel without seeing souls saved. The roots of present-day Assembly missionary outreach are to be found in the examples set by such men as A.N. Groves, Dan Crawford and F.S. Arnot.

How highly do we value this heritage? In spite of the dissensions and bitterness which marred the movement, it is an inspiring story. There is always a tendency to depart from the basic truths which were held so dearly by the founders of any movement. We need constantly to check our practices and attitudes, in order to ensure that we are remaining true to our wonderful heritage.

Let each reader search his or her heart with such questions as these:

Do I promote unity, and desire it above everything else?

Am I a cause, or encourager, of division?

While recognizing the impossibility of undoing the past, within the compass of my local Assembly, do I build up, or do I tear apart?

Do I love the Word, and give it its deserved place in personal and corporate life?

Do I have a spiritual appreciation of the Lord's Supper?

Do I sincerely prepare my heart for it, and partake of it, as often as it is possible for me to do so?

Does the teaching concerning the Lord's return constitute a vital factor in my thinking and in my life-style?

Do I have a deep commitment to the spreading of the Gospel?

If we value the legacy which we have received, we must endeavor, with genuine humility, to give honest answers to the foregoing questions. Before the Lord we must strive to rid our hearts of all traces of insincerity and arrogance, and accept it as our solemn responsibility to guard these precious Biblical teachings, until our Lord calls us to Himself.

# 2. The Lord's Supper

For a study of this topic, the key passage of Scripture is 1 Corinthians 11:20-29.

*20 When ye come together therefore into one place, this is not to eat the Lord's supper.*

*21 For in eating every one taketh before other his own supper: and one is hungry, and another is drunken.*

*22 What? have ye not houses to eat and to drink in? or despise ye the church of God, and shame them that have not? What shall I say to you? shall I praise you in this? I praise you not.*

*23 For I have received of the Lord that which also I delivered unto you, That the Lord Jesus the same night in which he was betrayed took bread:*

*24 And when he had given thanks, he brake it, and said, Take, eat: this is my body, which is broken for you: this do in remembrance of me.*

*25 After the same manner also he took the cup, when he had supped, saying, This cup is the new testament in my blood: this do ye, as oft as ye drink it, in remembrance of me.*

*26 For as often as ye eat this bread, and drink this cup, ye do shew the Lord's death till he come.*

*27 Wherefore whosoever shall eat this bread, and drink this cup of the Lord, unworthily, shall be guilty of the body and blood of the Lord.*

*28 But let a man examine himself, and so let him eat of that bread, and drink of that cup.*

*29 For he that eateth and drinketh unworthily, eateth and drinketh damnation to himself, not discerning the Lord's body.*

The expression 'The Lord's Supper' is not one which occurs frequently in the New Testament. Indeed, the opening sentence of the above passage contains its only occurrence in the King James Version. Another title is found in the Acts of the Apostles; – 'The Breaking of Bread' (Acts 2:42) In certain ecclesiastical circles, terms such as 'Communion'; 'Holy Communion' and 'The Eucharist' are employed, but we need not delay now to explain the peculiar significance of these.

A more useful exercise is to attempt to go back to the roots of the subject. In the previous chapter, we have been reminded of how 'the early Brethren' earnestly desired to go right back to what the Bible taught. For us, today, there is no better course. Our beliefs and practices must always be tested by what is written in the infallible Word of God.

To guide us in this particular study, there are four accounts of the institution of the Supper, upon which we can base our conclusions. These are found in Matthew 26, Mark 14, Luke 22 and 1 Corinthians 11. We believe that all of these are Divinely inspired and are, therefore, of equal importance, but perhaps a special significance attaches itself to the 1 Corinthians passage in that it is the oldest record of what our Lord said and did on that occasion. (It is generally accepted that the Corinthian account pre-dates those of Matthew, Mark and Luke.)

First of all, then, let us consider:

## 1. The Setting of the Supper

1 Corinthians 11:23 leaves us in no doubt as to when the Lord's Supper was introduced. The noteworthy words are ... "the Lord Jesus the same night in which he was betrayed, took bread ..." We picture in our minds the large, upstairs room, the table and the benches; we witness the Lord and His men assembled there; we recall His wonderful words to them, recorded for us in John 13-16, and we try to capture something of the very special atmosphere which filled the room as He laid aside His garments, and proceeded to perform a slave's duties

in the washing of their feet. Such was the setting for the introduction of the Supper.

The primary reason, of course, for their assembling that evening was to celebrate the Passover. As far as the time factor goes, the Passover and the Lord's Supper are very closely linked. As they ate the one, the other was introduced. We must not, however, confuse the one with the other. The Passover is Jewish, whereas the Lord's Supper is Christian. Even at the time of which we are thinking, the Passover was long-established, having been celebrated since the days of Moses, whereas the Supper was new. The Passover is an annual event; the Lord's Supper is a weekly event. (See Acts 20:7) The Passover is, to a large degree, family-based, in contrast to which the Lord's Supper is church-based. (Note the emphasis in 1 Corinthians 11 on 'coming together'.)

In addition to noting differences between the Passover and the Lord's Supper, it is also interesting to observe points of similarity between the two. For example, both are retrospective. Whenever a Jewish family celebrates Passover, they are looking backwards to their historic deliverance from Egypt. We, in participating in the Lord's Supper are looking back to Calvary and recalling the great spiritual deliverance effected for us by our Lord Jesus, in His suffering and death.

Furthermore, both are educative. Right down to the present time, the Passover is an excellent educational 'tool'. It was so designed by the Lord that it would inform little children about their glorious history. (See Exodus 12:25-27) Their questions were not to be ignored, but were to be answered by reference to the details of the Feast. Likewise, the Supper offers to all who thoughtfully observe its celebration, precious and wonderful insights into the significance of our Lord's death. It is difficult to think of any greater visual presentation of Gospel truth than that which is available at the Lord's Supper, and for this reason Christian parents should ensure that their off-spring are present (as observers) at the Supper, from as early an age as possible.

Both the Passover and the Lord's Supper have also a

prospective element. The lamb of Exodus 12, and of the subsequent Passovers in the centuries which followed, was a clear pointer to our Lord Jesus, the Lamb of God, who would be 'sacrificed for us' (1 Corinthians 5:7). With regard to the Lord's Supper, the prospective element lies in the fact that we participate of it 'till He come'.

It is evident then that there are note-worthy points both of difference and of similarity between the Passover and the Lord's Supper.

## 2. The Simplicity of the Supper

Whatever unresolved problems may remain in our minds with reference to the celebration of the Lord's Supper, we cannot fail to notice that, as far as the record of Scripture goes, there is a delightful simplicity.

The surroundings in which the Supper was instituted were simple; there was nothing ornate or elaborate about the furnishings of the room. In this particular, the 'early Brethren' were attempting to recover something which had been lost for many centuries. Today, we make it one of our aims to maintain this apostolic simplicity. This, of course, should not be advanced as an excuse or a reason for having shabby or untidy accommodation.

Likewise, the Lord's chosen symbols were simple. He "took bread...also he took the cup...". (1 Corinthians 11:23,25) How thankful we are that the Lord employed only bread and wine — substances that are readily available in every part of the habitable earth!

Our Lord's language was simple, too. "This is my body which is broken for you...this do in remembrance of me," were His words as He handed the bread to His disciples. Likewise with regard to the cup, He said, "This cup is the new testament in my blood: this do ye, as oft as ye drink it, in remembrance of me." We can be sure that His language was not intended to confuse or deceive, but rather, to impress upon the minds of His apostles the clarity of what He was saying and doing.

Human nature always has a tendency to embellish important, historical happenings with a halo of pageantry, ceremony and pomp. We must, therefore, ever be on our guard lest we should drift away from the original simplicity of the Supper.

## 3. The Sanctity of the Supper

It is very evident that serious disorders had come into the celebration of the Supper at Corinth. (See 1 Corinthians 11:20-22) It would seem that they were attempting to combine the Lord's Supper with a social occasion at which excesses, in the matters of food and drink, were being perpetrated. To further complicate the disorder, social and class distinctions amongst the church members were being accentuated. This, in turn, was creating a very fertile hot-bed for the propagation of heresies and divisions, of which the church at Corinth already had had considerable experience. It is no wonder, then, that Paul begins this section by saying, "When therefore ye assemble yourselves together, it is not possible to eat the Lord's Supper."(verse 20 R.V.)

Thankfully such excesses of gluttony and drunkenness are rare today amongst those who participate in the Supper. Nonetheless, the lessons are there for us to learn. A sense of reverence and an awareness of the sacredness of the occasion befit the Lord's Supper. Note how Paul calls for self-examination on the part of each one who partakes. (verse 28) We are to ensure that our lives are free from all known contradictions and inconsistencies. Every aspect of our behaviour is to be submitted to the Lordship of Christ. (Note how frequently 'the Lord' is mentioned in verses 23, 26, 27, 29, 32.) If we do so, we shall avoid the pitfalls into which the Corinthian church had fallen; a fitting atmosphere of reverence will pervade.

## 4. The Significance of the Supper

Behind the symbols there lies a deep spiritual significance of which we must never lose sight. The bread does not cease to be bread, neither does the cup of wine undergo any change of substance. There is no Scriptural foundation for the doctrine of transubstantiation, which teaches that after the bread has been consecrated, the body and blood, together with the soul and divinity of our Lord Jesus Christ, are contained 'truly, really and substantially in the sacrament of the most holy eucharist'. (See 'The New Unger's Bible Dictionary', 1988 edition, page 784) Neither this belief, nor the somewhat modified doctrine of consubstantiation, has a Biblical basis. We believe that when the Lord Jesus said, "This is my body;" He simply meant, "This represents my body."

It may be helpful to consider five aspects of the significance of the Lord's Supper.

1. It is AN ACT OF OBEDIENCE. Each believer, in partaking of the Supper, is obeying the Lord's command. In Matthew's account of its institution, the Lord used three commands:

'take', 'eat', and 'do'. In Mark's account, two commands are recorded: 'take' and 'eat'; while Luke mentions only one: 'do'. In Paul's account, as given us in 1 Corinthians 11, there are four imperatives: 'take', 'eat', 'do' and 'do'.

We all recognize that commands call for obedience, on our part. It may sound somewhat old-fashioned in today's world, but we believe that there can be no real spiritual progress in either individual life or in local church life, if we are not prepared to cultivate a spirit of whole-hearted and willing obedience to the Lord's commands. "To obey is better than sacrifice...", was the Lord's word to Saul, through the prophet Samuel. (1 Samuel 15:23) It may be that we are unable, through spiritual immaturity or mental limitation, to understand the full implications of the Lord's Supper, yet we should accept it at this basic level, and respond to His command, "This do ...".

2. It is AN ACT OF REMEMBRANCE. The ability to recall to mind persons and events is one of God's most precious gifts to us. With reference to the Supper, He says to us, "This do in remembrance of me." The word which He used denotes a bringing to mind, not a mere memory of Him. It is as though

He was saying, 'Here is a definite way by means of which I want you to bring Me back, positively and clearly, into your minds.' What a disappointment to our Lord, if He finds us unwilling to take time, in our busy lives, to 'do this for a remembrance of Me'! How grieving to His heart, if we allow trivial things to prevent us from taking our place at His Supper!

3. It is AN ACT OF FELLOWSHIP. This point is presented to us in 1 Corinthians 10:16,17:

> The cup of blessing which we bless, is it not the communion of the blood of Christ? The bread which we break, is it not the communion of the body of Christ? For we being many are one bread, and one body: for we are all partakers of that one bread.

The word 'communion' signifies 'having in common' or 'the share which one has in anything'. The apostle's questions in verse 16 are intended to focus our minds upon the fact that believers have fellowship in all that is the outcome of the death of Christ. We together share in the benefits of His body and blood. The fact that each believer takes a portion of the loaf for himself, is a symbolic way of showing that he, as an individual, has fellowship with Christ on the grounds of His death. The fact that all the believers do likewise is an expression of the essential oneness of the members of 'the body of Christ'. Thus our participation in the Lord's Supper is an expression of our personal 'sharing in' all that accrues from our Lord's suffering and death. In addition to this, however, it is an expression of our fellowship one with the other, inasmuch as all are partaking of the same loaf and drinking of the same cup.

Perhaps this concept of 'the communion of the body and blood of Christ' is the high-water mark of the significance of the Supper. How highly we ought to value opportunities for such fellowship!

4. It is AN ACT OF PROCLAMATION. In 1 Corinthians 11:26, the King James Version states, "As often as ye eat this bread and drink this cup, ye do show the Lord's death...". The Revised Version conveys the meaning more accurately by sub-

stituting 'proclaim' for 'show'; for such, indeed, is the meaning of the verb which Paul uses. The same word is used frequently of preaching, in the Acts of the Apostles. (See e.g., 4:2,13:5) The Revised Version consistently renders it as 'proclaim'.

In the celebration of the Lord's Supper, apart altogether from whatever words we may utter, there is a very eloquent proclamation of the fact, the significance, and the effectiveness of His death.

*'No Gospel like this feast,*
*Spread for us, Lord, by Thee;*
*No prophet nor evangelist*
*Preach the glad news so free.'*

5. It is AN ACT OF ANTICIPATION. The 'proclamation' is to continue "till He come." (verse 26) Here is clear proof that the Lord's Supper was never to be regarded as a temporary institution, of significance only in apostolic times. Each occasion of its celebration is designed to keep the hope of His return bright in the minds and hearts of His people. Week by week, thoughts are turned backwards to recall His sufferings and death, and also forwards to anticipate His coming again. When that great event takes place, the remembrance will cease, for His people will be with Him, in a sense hitherto unknown. The need for symbols will no longer exist.

We do not know when the Rapture will take place, but let us all be strengthened in our resolve to avail ourselves of this precious love-gift which He has given us —'The Lord's Supper'.

*'Keep the holy Feast with gladness,*
*Love's redeeming work is done:*
*Showing forth His death of sadness,*
*Breaking bread — until He come'.*

# 3. The Priesthood of Believers

Two important passages of Scripture relating to the topic of the priesthood of believers are:

## 1 Peter 2:5-9

*5   Ye also, as lively stones, are built up a spiritual house, an holy priesthood, to offer up spiritual sacrifices, acceptable to God by Jesus Christ.*

*6   Wherefore also it is contained in the scripture, Behold, I lay in Sion a chief corner stone, elect, precious: and he that believeth on him shall not be confounded.*

*7   Unto you therefore which believe he is precious: but unto them which be disobedient, the stone which the builders disallowed, the same is made the head of the corner,*

*8   And a stone of stumbling, and a rock of offence, even to them which stumble at the word, being disobedient: whereunto also they were appointed.*

*9   But ye are a chosen generation, a royal priesthood, an holy nation, a peculiar people; that ye should shew forth the praises of him who hath called you out of darkness into his marvellous light:*

## Revelation 1:4-6

*4   John to the seven churches which are in Asia: Grace be unto you, and peace, from him which is, and which was, and which is to come; and from the seven Spirits which are before his throne;*

*5   And from Jesus Christ, who is the faithful witness, and the first begotten of the dead, and the prince of the kings of the earth. Unto him that loved us, and washed us from our sins in his own blood,*

*6 And hath made us kings and priests unto God and his Father; to him be glory and dominion for ever and ever. Amen.*

As an introduction to the subject, it may be useful to remind ourselves that the Scriptures use a wide variety of names for Christians. For example, they are called 'saints', 'ambassadors' and 'children', amongst others. These are figurative, or pictorial, ways of defining our relationship with God our Father, and with our Lord Jesus Christ. Each term presents a distinctive aspect of truth, and we have the responsibility of comparing one passage of Scripture with another, in order to unfold the particular teaching conveyed by any given description.

Our present task is to focus on yet another New Testament name for Christians, 'priests'. We shall ask, and endeavour to find Biblical answers to, three questions:

1. Who are priests in this age?
2. What does it mean to be a priest?
3. What are the functions of a priest?

In considering the first question, we must divest our minds of all concepts which we may have formed as a result of our cultural or ecclesiastical associations in earlier life. For example, I, with a Northern Ireland upbringing, would only have envisaged a priest as a 'father' or 'minister' of the Roman Catholic chapel. To my boyish mind, such a man was easily recognized in public by his distinctive garb.

Such notions, however, are put aside when we come to the Word of God, for therein it is clearly taught that every one who is a believer in the Lord Jesus Christ is a priest. The priesthood of believers is unconnected with seminary training, human ordination and appointment, or with a special kind of dress.

In support of this position, we turn to 1 Peter 2, where

Peter addresses a body of Christians, and tells them that they are both a "holy priesthood" and a "royal priesthood". Revelation 1:5,6 is also a very significant passage: having been "washed from our sins", we have been constituted "kings and priests unto God". There is no evidence to suggest that Peter is addressing a privileged class within the Christian community. He is not singling out one group of believers and giving them a status which is denied to others. On the contrary, what he is saying applies to all the believers, from the youngest to the oldest, and from the least instructed one right through to the most mature one. The idea of a sacerdotal or priestly class, which exercises functions forbidden to other believers, is entirely foreign to the New Testament.

The truth of the priesthood of believers is one of the doctrines recovered by the 'early Brethren' at the beginning of the nineteenth century. It came with a great sense of relief and freedom to their minds and hearts. Groves spoke of it as 'the removal of a mountain'. They affirmed that all believers are true, spiritual priests, fitted and privileged by Divine grace to enter into God's presence and offer spiritual sacrifices without any interposition of any man, apart from the one Mediator, the Lord Jesus Christ. The commonly accepted distinction between 'clergy' and 'laity' was, therefore, hurtful to them.

Perhaps a balanced understanding of the New Testament's teaching on the priesthood of believers can be grasped most easily if we picture a local church situation where a company of Christians has gathered for the celebration of the Lord's Supper. Every one of them, whether brother or sister, is a priest. In that regard, they are all equal. If, however, we examine their positions in relation to leadership or spiritual gift, we at once recognise that there are differences. They are not all equal in respect of positions of responsibility in the assembly. Equality in priesthood does not imply equality in 'gift', or in elderhood.

Furthermore, the New Testament teaches us that men and women priests do not operate in identical ways in the local church. The 'men-priests' participate in a public way, audibly bringing the worship and praise of the assembled company to the Lord, whereas the 'women-priests' are in silence, as far as leading in worship and teaching are concerned. (See 1 Corinthians 14:34 and 1 Timothy 2:11,12.) This is not to say that their worship and praise are one whit less pleasing to the Lord. Acceptance of God's ordained 'modus operandi' does not diminish the volume of worship ascending to Him! (The matter of the respective roles of brothers and sisters is dealt with more fully in a subsequent chapter.)

## 2. What does it mean to be a priest?

In endeavouring to understand what it means to be a priest, we must allow our thinking to be regulated by the Word of God, and not by either historical or contemporary ideas. The Oxford English Dictionary, for example, defines a priest as "a minister of the altar, especially an officiant at the Eucharist" or, "one above a deacon ... and below a bishop, with authority to administer the Sacraments, and pronounce absolution." It is immediately obvious that such ecclesiastical terminology does not harmonize with Biblical teaching. We must allow the Bible to be its own interpreter.

We are on much surer ground when we go back to the Old Testament, and discover there what it meant to be a priest. Take the situation envisaged in Leviticus chapter 1. An Israelite is approaching the gate of the Tabernacle, leading a bullock which he wishes to offer as a burnt offering to the Lord. We will assume that his animal is "without blemish", as the law stipulates in verse 3, and that he himself is a godly Israelite who is making this offering to the Lord "of his own voluntary will." He is not a criminal, nor is he consciously aware, on his part, of any violation of God's law; his desire, simply, is to express his appreciation of the Lord by means of the sacrifice of his bullock.

As we observe the proceedings, we will undoubtedly be impressed by the fact that the offerer is very restricted in how far he is permitted to go, in his approach to the Tabernacle. Indeed, he cannot proceed beyond "the door of the Tabernacle". (verse 3) At that point, he must stop and await the services of the priests who are on duty on that particular day. They will perform their part in bringing the blood to the altar and in sprinkling it there. They, too, will make the fire of the altar ready to receive the bullock's body when the offerer has completed the skinning and the cutting. This done, the priests will lay all the parts, in the appropriate order, upon the altar where it will all be consumed as "an offering made by fire, of a sweet savour unto the Lord." (verse 9) All the while, the offerer keeps his distance — he has no entitlement to come near, or to assist the priests. Never for one moment would he contemplate taking over from them in the discharge of their duties!

Keeping in mind this picture of procedures in the days of the Aaronic priesthood, let us revert to the New Testament teaching which we have been considering. There is a remarkable contrast between the two! The whole emphasis in the instruction of the 1 Peter 2 passage is that we have no need of any human priest. The work of our Lord Jesus Christ is so perfect and complete, that we can come right into the very presence of God, without the services of any human intermediary. Each of us is a priest, and hence there is no need of a special order of men to act on our behalf, in our approach to God.

In response, then, to the question, 'What does it mean to be a priest?', we affirm that priesthood has to do with our access to God. This is based solely on the merit of our Lord Jesus Christ, and His offering for us. We come to God directly and apart altogether from any other intermediary, and we are assured of acceptance by Him. The words of Hebrews 10:19-22 are particularly relevant: "Having therefore, brethren, boldness to enter into the holiest by the blood of Jesus, by a new and living way, which he hath consecrated for us, through the veil, that is to say, his flesh; and having an high priest over the house of God; let us draw near with a true heart in full assurance of faith, having our hearts sprinkled from an evil conscience, and our bodies washed with pure water." In the light of this, let us not be negligent in availing ourselves of our blood-bought privilege. "Let us come boldly to the throne of grace..." Hebrews 4:16.

Perhaps at this point it would be helpful to examine briefly the historical development of the role of the priest throughout the Scriptures. If we go back to the earliest times, and examine priesthood in the days of the patriarchs (such as Abraham, Isaac and Jacob), we shall find that the head of the family acted as priest on behalf of his offspring, and indeed, of his household. (See e.g., Genesis chs.18, 28 and 49)

Following the Exodus, under Moses, God declared His intention to constitute Israel as 'a kingdom of priests'. (See Exodus 19:6) This, however, was conditional, for the promise of national priesthood was prefaced with the words, "If ye will obey my voice indeed, and keep my covenant...' (verse 5). It is abundantly clear that Israel failed to obey, and following their gross idolatry in the matter of the golden calf (Exodus 32), God chose the family of Aaron for the duties of priesthood. Aaron himself became the High Priest, and his sons served in lesser roles. Thus was introduced a selective, hereditary priesthood, which continued in some form or other, right down to the first century.

Upon the death of the Lord Jesus, you will recall that the veil of the Temple was rent from the top to the bottom. This miraculous happening was God's method of signifying that the old order was finished and a new order was being introduced. Henceforth, every believer belongs to the holy and royal priesthood of which Peter has written. ( 1 Peter 2) The Lord Jesus, having perfectly accomplished His work of atonement, "by his own blood entered in once into the holy place...." (Hebrews 9:12) In Him, every believer has access, and we are urged to approach God for ourselves. How thankful we should be that what the law did not accomplish, grace has!

This precious truth was, to some extent, revived in the days of the fifteenth century Reformation. Martin Luther, who was awakened to realize the errors of the Roman priesthood, wrote, "All Christians are altogether priests; he who says otherwise says it without the Word of God, on no authority but the sayings and customs of men." We have also seen that it was a firm conviction of the 'early Brethren' in the beginning of the nineteenth century.

### 3. What are the functions of a priest?

In the first place, his function is to offer sacrifices. Hebrews 5:1 speaks of Israel's high priest as one who is "ordained for men in things pertaining to God, that he may offer both gifts and sacrifices for sins." We have seen that in the Old Testament times, the sacrifices were animals, but in 1 Peter 2:5 we are instructed that for the 'holy priesthood' of today, they are of a spiritual nature.

A careful examination of the New Testament will enable us to identify several kinds of 'spiritual sacrifices' which we may offer. Perhaps foremost in our thinking should be the presentation of our bodies, as Romans 12:1 enjoins us. By 'your body' the writer is conveying the idea of 'your whole person'. Because of the comprehensiveness of Christ's redeeming work, God has a claim upon us in the totality of our beings, and we ought not to hold back any department of our lives, or any aspect of our personalities from the altar of sacrifice.

With hearts broken and contrite because of our sinfulness, yet ever deeply appreciative of the work of Calvary, we could usefully employ Frances Ridley Havergal's words:

*Take my life, and let it be*
*Consecrated, Lord, to Thee.*
*Take my hands, and let them move*
*At the impulse of Thy love.*

Another aspect of our 'spiritual sacrifices' is the offering of praise. Hebrews 13:15 encourages us in this direction. "By him therefore let us offer the sacrifice of praise to God continually, that is, the fruit of our lips giving thanks to his name." Right of entry into His presence is our exalted privilege, and how fitting it is that we should praise Him! The presentation of praise may assume several forms; it may be by singing, or as an element of our prayers, or even as an unuttered disposition of gratitude to the Lord, as we go about the varied tasks of our daily lives. "Whoso offereth praise glorifieth me." (Psalm 50:23) When we fail to do so, we deprive God of what is His due. Like the healed Samaritan leper, we should return "to give glory to God". (Luke 17:18)

In addition to our persons and our praise, it is likely that all of us have some possessions that we can present to God, as a part of our discharge of our priestly functions. The Hebrews 13 passage quoted above goes on to say, "But to do good and to communicate forget not: for with such sacrifices God is well pleased." (verse 16) (To communicate means 'to share with', and the thought is that what we share with others who are in need, is seen by the Lord as having been, first of all, presented to Him.) He accepts our giving of our material possessions as a sacrifice, well-pleasing to Him.

A second answer to the question, 'What are the functions of a priest?' is that he communicates something of the nature and character of God to men. It has often been said that believers are a 'holy priesthood' because they 'go in' to the presence of God with their spiritual sacrifices, and they are a 'royal priesthood' in that they 'go out' to "show forth the praises of him who hath called them out of darkness into his marvelous light". (1 Peter 2:5,9) Hence all true service for God is really priestly in character; we come from God to a needy world, mediating the love and grace of God to those who are in moral and spiritual darkness. When this is grasped, we come to understand that 'service' and 'worship' are not very far apart, for worship is the direct acknowledgment of God in His nature, His ways and His claims upon us. We worship Him, either by the outpouring of our hearts in praise and thanksgiving, or by actions which in themselves are the very expression of what we know God to be.

Local church life affords many opportunities for the exercise of priestly functions CORPORATELY. We meet, for example, on the Lord's Day to remember the Lord in the breaking of bread and in drinking the cup. It is conceded that this meeting is nowhere in Scripture called 'The Worship Meeting', yet surely it will be agreed that it is at this meeting our worship should reach its highest corporate level. Much depends upon our individual spiritual condition. If we are not worshipping personally, shall we be able to worship corporately?

If we come together as individual priests, with hearts and minds attuned to the purpose for which we have assembled, then the Spirit of God can direct the corporate worship of the company. As one brother after another rises to his feet to lead the gathering, it should be understood that he is speaking representatively. He is presenting to God, as it were, the accumulated worship of the entire body of worshippers. As the others listen, they are acquiescing in their hearts, and perhaps, in silence, are adding their own contributions to that precious, fragrant incense which is going up to God.

One of our greatest needs today is for brethren to exercise their priestly privileges at the Lord's Supper. God will be magnified and our gatherings will be greatly enriched, if we have men whose hearts are full of the greatness of Christ, and who are ready, under the guidance of the Holy Spirit, to present to God, on behalf of the company, their sincere appreciation of the work and the worth of the Lord Jesus.

*Lamb of God, through Thee we enter*
*Inside the veil;*
*Cleansed by Thee, we boldly venture*
*Inside the veil:*
*Not a stain; a new creation;*
*Ours is such a full salvation;*
*Low we bow in adoration*
*Inside the veil.*

## 4. The Family and the Assembly

### Ephesians 5:20-25,28

*20   Giving thanks always for all things unto God and the Father in the name of our Lord Jesus Christ;*

*21   Submitting yourselves one to another in the fear of God.*

*22   Wives, submit yourselves unto your own husbands, as unto the Lord.*

*23   For the husband is the head of the wife, even as Christ is the head of the church: and he is the saviour of the body.*

*24   Therefore as the church is subject unto Christ, so let the wives be to their own husbands in every thing.*

*25   Husbands, love your wives, even as Christ also loved the church, and gave himself for it;*

*28   So ought men to love their wives as their own bodies. He that loveth his wife loveth himself.*

### Ephesians 6:1-4

*1   Children, obey your parents in the Lord: for this is right.*

*2   Honour thy father and mother; (which is the first commandment with promise;)*

*3   That it may be well with thee, and thou mayest live long on the earth.*

*4   And, ye fathers, provoke not your children to wrath: but bring them up in the nurture and admonition of the Lord.*

It is evident from the letters of the New Testament that first century churches were comprised of all age-groups. In support of this statement, we note references in 1 Timothy to 'younger men', 'elders', 'elder women', 'younger women'; and in Ephesians to 'children'. It is also clear that the component members of a local church were often related to each other by natural ties. Thus, Ephesians 5 has instruction for husbands and wives, and Ephesians 6 contains teaching for fathers and children. In 1 Timothy 5 there is instruction which relates to three generations of the one family, – if we accept the Revised Version rendering of verse 4. We also note that in some churches there were 'households' (See e.g., Romans 16:10, 2 Timothy 4:19), and while the term 'household' may include house-servants, it is likely that natural family members are also meant.

All this leads us to the conclusion that God's intention is that local church life should be the spiritual base of Christian families. What a joy it is to see perhaps three generation of the one family sitting down together, along with other believers, to remember the Lord!

In 1 Thessalonians, Paul uses language that points to the close links which exist between family and assembly. We note his use of two significant similes. In 2:7 he says, "But we were gentle among you, as when a nurse cherisheth her own children". (See R.V. ) Here the picture of a loving, nursing mother is used to portray the care necessary for the nurturing of "babes in Christ". (1 Corinthians 3:1) Then, in 2:11, he reminds the Thessalonian believers that "we exhorted and comforted and charged every one of you, as a father doth his children", suggesting that fatherly words of caution and firmness are just as appropriate in the spiritual life of the assembly as they are in the natural life of the family.

It is apparent, then, that in the mind of God there are links between family and assembly. Indeed, both owe their existence to Him. God is the Creator of family-life. His very first words to the couple whom He had made were, "Be fruitful and multiply...' (Genesis 1:28) Likewise, the concept of local churches, or assemblies is divine in origin. In Revelation 1-3, they are likened to 'golden lampstands', gold being suggestive of their heavenly origin. In addition, they are referred to, individually, as 'the house of God', 'the church of God' and 'the temple of God'. (See 1 Timothy 3:15, 1 Corinthians 1:2 and 3:16)

It follows, therefore, that when we speak about Christian families and New Testament churches, we are considering matters to which a peculiar sacredness is attached. Besides, the one has an impact upon the other. If Christian families lose their distinctiveness and become patterned after the standards of the ungodly world, there will inevitably follow a weakening of the spiritual vitality of the assembly. Conversely, healthy local assemblies, where the standards of the Word of God are lovingly and faithfully taught and practised, cannot fail to contribute to the consolidation of Christian homes.

We are all keenly aware that both institutions — family and assembly — are coming under heavy Satanic attack. In today's world, there are many factors which can very easily wreak havoc upon a Christian family. Never at any time in Christian history were there more broken marriages and separated families than at the present time. None of us can calculate the pain, the heart-break, the tears and sorrow which have accrued from such break-downs. Running almost in tandem with this, there exist much coldness, division, strife and jealousy which are sapping away the vigour of assembly-life. How we long to recover the power and freshness of the early nineteenth century, to say nothing of the vitality of the first century!

If we sincerely desire to build both solid Christian families, and strong New Testament patterned assemblies, we must make it our solemn resolve to be guided only by the Word. As we come to the Scriptures to find what God requires, we discover that His demands in the one area are not really very different from His requirements in the other. There is not one set of moral standards for family-life; and another, different set for assembly-life. No sharp dichotomy exists between the two; indeed, in many regards the latter is an extension of the former. The values and criteria of the Christian home are developed and amplified on the wider canvas of the local church.

Take, for example, the quality of love. In a Christian family, this must be indisputably the foremost quality. True Christian love will be in evidence in the various relationships within the family — the love of husband for wife; the devoted self-sacrificing of parents for children; the respect and obedience of children towards parents. There cannot be anything more important in Christian families than this. It will constantly undergird the Christian home in all the strains and stresses imposed upon it as children develop from infancy through to adolescence. In addition, love, in its Biblical sense, will form a bulwark against the evil external influences which assail the Christian family. There is much need in family-life for wisdom, forbearance, patience and understanding; these delicate 'plants' will flourish most successfully in the warm atmosphere of a Christ-like love.

Even a casual reading of the New Testament cannot fail to impress us with the emphasis laid upon the importance of love one for another in the context of church-life. All twenty-one letters of the New Testament refer to this matter, in some way or other. Perhaps it is the only topic alluded to so comprehensively! "See that ye love one another with a pure heart fervently," is Peter's word in 1 Peter 1:22, and in 4:8 he adds, "Above all things have fervent charity (love) among yourselves." How easy it is for us to allow the fire of love one for another to die down! We become so accustomed to each other, that we take each other for granted, to the extent of becoming critical and fault-finding. If coldness characterises the relationship between believers within the same local assembly, we need not be surprised if our families, as they grow up, fail to be attracted to it. They will quickly sense the deficiency and, in consequence, will seek a spiritual 'home' elsewhere. Let it be our constant endeavour, then, to maintain in both family and assembly that quality of love which is a clear reflection of the sacrificial love of our Lord Jesus.

Another feature which the Lord desires to find in both family and assembly is discipline. The essential idea behind this word is 'training', rather than the administering of punishment for misdemeanours. When understood in this sense, it will be seen that discipline in the family-context is an on-going matter. The normal routine of family-life constitutes a training ground in which children are being taught, both directly and indirectly, cardinal Christian virtues such as obedience, respect and unselfishness.

Ephesians chapter 6 lays the responsibility upon Christian fathers to bring their offspring up "in the nurture and admonition of the Lord." The word translated 'nurture' might be rendered 'chastening', as in the Revised Version. It is a word which denotes the training of a child, including instruction. Most of this training will take place informally in the day-by-day pattern of the home, and will be governed by the values and standards set by Christian parents. There ought, of course, to be features which mark the family as being distinctively 'Christian', as opposed to merely 'good'. In particular, it is in the reading of the Word of God and in family prayer, that the essential Christian element will be introduced into the home situation.

A feature of the times in which we are living is that the years of childhood are being perceptively foreshortened. The modern world, with its unashamed openness on matters which only a few decades ago would never have been mentioned in public, is snatching children from their 'sweet innocence' at an ever-earlier age. It is not possible to cocoon our children totally from the evils which characterise these 'last days' in which we live, nor can we bring them up as 'green-house plants', totally sheltered from the harsh winds of the real world. We must, therefore, make full use of their formative years, and seek to train them in the ways of the Lord, all the while looking earnestly to Him to do His unique work of salvation in their young lives.

The concept of discipline, or training, carries over from family to assembly. The local church is not 'a free-for-all', where one can act and speak as he or she pleases! As in the home, so in the church, authority is recognised and upheld. We are enjoined to obey those who have rule over us, and to submit to them. (See Hebrews 13:7,17) Assembly-life provides an arena where respect for another's opinions, patience with another's idiosyncrasies, and submission to Divinely appointed leadership are cultivated. It is a training ground, the ultimate goal being nothing less than the development of the Christ-like "fruit of the Spirit" in each member. (Galatians 5)

Another area common to both family and assembly is that of growth. In a Christian home, the spiritual growth of each member should be continuous. It is a sad situation if, through our negligence or apathy, our spiritual development has been arrested, and we find ourselves going through the motions of religious activities without having the joy and zest of our 'first love' permeating through us. We must guard carefully against the inroads of business, recreation and other demands, lest we find ourselves deprived of time for private devotions and communion with the Lord through His Word. We cannot nurture our families, if we, at a personal level, are starved of 'the Bread of life'.

There is a strong insistence in the New Testament that local churches should be spheres of spiritual growth. Through the public teaching of the Scriptures — "the sincere milk of the word", as 1 Peter 2:2 calls it — we grow. Upon the elders of the assembly devolves the solemn duty of feeding the Church of God over which the Holy Ghost has made them overseers. (See Acts 20:28) God's intention for His people is that they do not remain at the 'baby-stage', but that they "grow up into him in all things." (Ephesians 4:15) This objective is achievable, not merely by personal spiritual growth in the home and family, but by the corporate experience available to us through whole-hearted commitment to local church membership.

A Christian family will also be marked by a genuine concern for other people. The love exhibited in the family will not be entirely inward-looking, restricting itself to its own family members. Circumstances will, of course, vary from home to home, but Christian families will strive to show the love of Christ in practical ways to others where need exists. It may be to a neighbour who is ill, or aged, or perhaps at a time of bereavement. Opportunities will arise, too, for acts of good neighbourliness in very practical matters. In all such cases, an excellent example is being set for young children who observe their parents thus showing thoughtfulness and love towards those in need.

Moving from family to assembly, there should be no less-ening, but rather an intensifying of sincere concern for others. We are "to do good to all men, but especially to them which are of the household of faith." (Galatians 6:10) The Scriptures present us with an extensive range of injunctions, the cumula-tive effect of which is to impress upon us that we are to steer completely away from a selfish, self-centered life-style, and to develop, instead, a concern for others. Think, for example, of these: –

| | |
|---|---|
| "Serve one another" | Galatians 5:13 |
| "Bear one another's burdens" | Galatians 6:2 |
| "Comfort one another" | 1 Thessalonians 4:18 |
| "Use hospitality one to another" | 1 Peter 4:9 |
| "Be kind one to another" | Ephesians 4:32 |
| "Consider one another" | Hebrews 10:24 |

The New Testament also records for our instruction and encouragement examples of corporate relief schemes which were put in place to alleviate the suffering of others, often in distant parts. (See e.g., Acts 11 and 2 Corinthians.)

Not very far removed from the foregoing is another impor-tant link between family and assembly. It is what may be spo-ken of as a consistent witness to the name of the Lord Jesus. A solid Christian family sheds the light and truth of the Gospel to those around it. Its first responsibility, of course, is inward; little children must be taught their need of repentance and faith in the Lord Jesus. Diligently and consistently they must be instructed in the great teachings of the Word of God, at a level suited to their own stage of understanding.

The responsibility for Gospel-witness then widens to those around about. This may be done openly, perhaps by the distri-bution of literature, or by the display of Scripture texts. A less public means is by one-to-one witnessing, as opportunity aris-es. Whatever the method used, of supreme importance is the necessity for behaviour at all times to be in accord with Biblical standards; otherwise, even our best efforts will have no impact.

What marks the family should also mark the local church. All assemblies should be 'gospel-minded', like those at Philippi and Thessalonica. Concerning the former, we read that they were "holding forth the word of life" (2:16), and the latter was commended for the fact that from them "sounded out the word of the Lord." (1:8) In today's prevailing climate of indifference and skepticism, it is extremely difficult to interest people in God's message of 'Good News', but we must not allow this to become an excuse for our slackness in evangelism.

Perhaps enough has been said to make the point that family and assembly should ideally be pursuing similar objectives. While each has its distinctives, the values and the standards upheld in the one apply very largely to the other. Young people, in particular, will be very quick to observe any inconsistencies between the two, and can be stumbled very easily by incompatible or hypocritical practices.

Godly parents, who desire only God's best for their offspring, will look for evidence, not only of salvation by grace alone, but also of growing convictions regarding the assembly principles which they themselves have held. It is as the qualities outlined above are fostered in the development of our young children that the seeds of such convictions will be sown in their hearts. Our earnest prayer and expectation will be that, in the goodness and mercy of God, bridges will be built from family to assembly. As in all cases of bridge-building, solid and enduring foundations are needed at both ends, so the future well-being of our children requires both strong Christian homes and stable, well-grounded, assemblies. If the spiritual tone of either is undermined by the unrelenting assaults of Satan, we can be sure that much harm is being done to the rising generation. Strong Christian families are an invaluable adjunct to strong Christian churches; conversely, families, weakened by worldliness or unfaithfulness can only result in assemblies bearing Laodicean features — "wretched, and miserable, and poor, and blind, and naked". (Revelation 3:17)

# 5. Money and Stewardship

### 1 Cor. 4:1,2

1   Let a man so account of us, as of the ministers of Christ, and stewards of the mysteries of God.

2   Moreover it is required in stewards, that a man be found faithful.

### 1 Cor.16:1-3

1   Now concerning the collection for the saints, as I have given order to the churches of Galatia, even so do ye.

2   Upon the first day of the week let every one of you lay by him in store, as God hath prospered him, that there be no gatherings when I come.

3   And when I come, whomsoever ye shall approve by your letters, them will I send to bring your liberality unto Jerusalem.

### 2 Cor. 9:6

6   But this I say, He which soweth sparingly shall reap also sparingly; and he which soweth bountifully shall reap also bountifully.

### 1 Peter 4:9,10

9   Use hospitality one to another without grudging.

10   As every man hath received the gift, even so minister the same one to another, as good stewards of the manifold grace of God.

The subject of money is one which figures very largely in the minds of men and women everywhere. Like fire, money can be a very excellent servant, or a terrible master.

## MONEY AND STEWARDSHIP

*Dug from the mountain-side, washed in the glen*
*Servant am I, or the master of men;*
*Steal me, I curse you; earn me, I bless you;*
*Grasp me and hoard me — a fiend shall possess you;*
*Live for me, die for me, covet me, take me —*
*Angel or devil, I am what you make me.'*

In considering the topic, we may usefully break it into three parts. First of all, there is the matter of acquiring money. We pass then to the stage of having money, which, in turn, leads on to using money.

In the first place, then, consider the *acquiring of money.* There are numerous ways by which people procure money, some of them undoubtedly honest and praiseworthy, others of questionable integrity! The normal and most common method is by work. For a believer in the Lord Jesus Christ, daily employment should be of such a character that it does not in any way conflict with the principles of his Christian faith. In today's harsh economic conditions, jobs may not be easily found. Nevertheless a Christian who has set his heart upon pleasing the Lord in all things, will think carefully about whatever job opportunities may present themselves to him. He will wish to be satisfied in his conscience that a particular job is entirely consistent with his standing as a believer. A relevant Bible passage is found in Titus chapter 3; verse 8 reads, "They which have believed in God might be careful to maintain good works." Perhaps the force of the verse becomes clearer in the Revised Version: "They which have believed in God may be careful to profess honest trades."

Reference has been made to John Nelson Darby, the outstanding classical scholar and linguist of the early nineteenth century, whom God used so mightily in the recovery of much Biblical truth. When he was a young man, he studied to become a lawyer, and was called to the Irish Chancery Bar, but because of his deep religious convictions he became uneasy about continuing in the legal profession. The upshot of the matter was that he resigned from the Bar on grounds of conscience. This is not to infer that all lawyers, solicitors and attorneys are deficient in integrity! In Darby's case, it was a matter of personal conviction before God, and he was unwilling to compromise his Christian principles for the sake of worldly gain.

Having found employment which will not conflict with our Christian profession, it is important for believers to develop and maintain a positive attitude towards their daily task. Work is honourable, for it is God's appointment for mankind whom He has created. The opening chapters of Genesis indicate that work pre-dates man's fall, and we ought not, therefore, to think of work as a form of punishment which has been imposed upon us because of Adam's disobedience. Before the first act of transgression occurred, we read that, "the Lord God took the man, and put him in the garden of Eden to dress it and to keep it." (Genesis 2:15) In the light of this, we must always endeavour to view our employment as a God-given opportunity to co-operate with Him in advancing His plans, both for ourselves and for His world.

The New Testament writings also encourage a healthy attitude towards work. In the Thessalonian church it appears that some men, able-bodied and of working-age, had abandoned their employment, and were leading idle lives. (Perhaps they had become so excited about the imminence of the Lord's return that they felt there was no necessity to engage in such a mundane affair as daily work!) In 2 Thessalonians chapter 3 Paul had stern words for them, even to the point of telling them that if they would not work, neither should they eat. He reminded them, too, of the fine example which he and his fellow apostles had given them, when they were with them — "neither did we eat any man's bread for nought, but wrought with labour and travail night and day, that we might not be chargeable to any of you." (See 2 Thessalonians 3:6-15) The whole Christian ethos with reference to work is summed up in Colossians 3:23, "And whatsoever ye do, do it heartily, as to the Lord, and not unto men."

Secondly, then, consider the Christian's attitude to *having, or owning, money.* Having been in employment, we are now in the position where we receive a wage or salary, and the question we now face is, 'What should my attitude be towards this wealth which I have acquired?'

Basically, there are two possible attitudes. The first of these expresses the view that what I have earned is absolutely mine, to be disposed of as I wish, and no one has any right to question my use of it. This is perhaps an over-simplification of the attitude of multitudes of people in the world today. It does, however, express the basic philosophy of the self-centered, materialistic society in which we live our lives.

The other possible approach involves the introduction into our thinking of the Biblical concept of stewardship. We recognize ourselves as 'stewards' of whatever wealth we have. By this we mean that we are 'managers' of another's possessions, for a steward is simply a person who is looking after something on behalf of, and in the interests of, the true owner. The idea is introduced at an early point in the Bible story; we read for example, about Abraham's steward (Genesis 15:2), and Joseph's steward (Genesis 43:19). It is very evident that both Abraham and Joseph were men of very considerable substance, and they employed stewards who managed their affairs for them. The stewards were, of course, accountable to their superiors for the manner in which they discharged their duties.

Transferring the notion of stewardship now from the material realm to the spiritual, we can readily grasp that Christian stewardship views money (and, indeed, all that we possess) as being the Lord's. What I have really belongs to Him, yet He has entrusted it to me, not to become mine as an absolute right, but, rather, to be used by me in a manner which will glorify Him and promote His interests.

In Old Testament days, King David accumulated a great quantity of materials for the building of the Temple. The actual construction was carried out by David's son, Solomon, but David was deeply involved in the gathering of the materials, and he was greatly moved by the willingness of the people to give. In his prayer of thanksgiving to the Lord, he said, "But who am I, and what is my people, that we should be able to offer so willingly after this sort? for all things come of thee, and of thine own have we given thee." (1 Chronicles 29:14) David recognized that God is the source of everything; in His grace and wisdom He had committed much to His people, and when they gave materials for the construction of the Temple, they were really only giving back to God what belonged to Him. David's understanding in this matter accords perfectly with the later development of the doctrine of Christian stewardship.

Our Lord's 'Parable of the Pounds' in Luke 19, reinforces the teaching. To each of ten servants was entrusted a pound, and their lord's instruction was, "Occupy till I come." There followed a period of absence on the part of the nobleman, during which time the servants were expected to be mindful of his injunction and busy themselves on his behalf. Eventually the nobleman returned and individually the servants were called to give an account. Remarkably, each one, when he addressed his master said, "Lord, THY pound ...". None of them spoke about "MY pound"... ! The fact of the matter is that they understood clearly that the pounds which had been handed over to them were not outright 'gifts', but were 'deposits' with which they were expected to trade in their lord's interests.

One servant, however, failed completely to use what had been entrusted to him. It had lain, carefully wrapped in a cloth, and unused, during the whole period of the nobleman's absence, and when the master returned, there was nothing to present to him, except his original pound! It must have been a moment of much regret for that servant, as he stood empty-handed before his master! Let us not miss its pointed message. To each of us the Lord has committed, not only material wealth, but also capabilities of varying kinds. Today He is 'absent'; soon He will return, and our lives will come under review at His judgmentseat. (See Romans 14:10 and 2 Corinthians 5:10) How tragic for us if at that day we have to admit that we wasted our time and opportunities, and failed to put to good use what the Lord had entrusted to us!

In the third place, we shall now consider the matter of *using money*. Assuming that we have accepted the Biblical teaching of stewardship, what principles are to govern our use of whatever money we have?

A very obvious, yet important, initial consideration is that we must discharge all our legal obligations. This will encompass our bills and taxes, in addition to all the ongoing expenses associated with the maintenance of a home and the upbringing of a family. The Scriptures caution us against falling into debt. "Owe no man anything," says Romans 13:8, while the preceding chapter instructs us to "provide things honest in the sight of all men." (verse 17)

The question will inevitably arise as to what standard of living we should strive after. Are we to have the very latest in everything as it becomes available? What degree of luxury should we permit ourselves in our homes? Are we to be motivated by a spirit of 'keeping up with the Jones's'? In offering answers to such questions as these, one must beware of adopting a legalistic, or hypocritical stance. Scope must be left for each individual believer to reach his own conclusions, having had his mind and heart instructed in the Biblical principles of stewardship. In the matter of providing for the necessities of life for both ourselves and our dependents, we are left in no doubt. "If any provide not for his own, and especially for those of his own house, he hath denied the faith, and is worse than an infidel." (1 Timothy 5:8)

When all the necessities have been taken care of, the question of 'extras' and luxuries remains. In this area, the pressure of the materialistic age impinges heavily upon us. Our Lord, in His teaching in Luke 12, cut right across the commonly-held values which govern men's thinking. "A man's life," He said, "consisteth not in the abundance of the things which he possesseth." (verse 15) In a world where a person's success and importance are judged by the abundance of his material possessions, our Lord's teaching should provide a necessary counter-balance. "Is not the life more than meat, and the body than raiment?" (Matthew 6:25)

At this point it might be appropriate to remind ourselves that the 'early Brethren', of whom we have spoken earlier, were characterized by an unworldliness to which many other Christian people were attracted. In many very practical ways, they sought to show that they were "strangers and pilgrims on the earth." (Hebrews 11:13) Their lives were simple. John Parnell, who became Lord Congelton, in his early days rented a working-man's house at £12 per year, and lived in great simplicity. When R.C. Chapman went to Barnstable, he too, rented a small house in a street of workmen's dwellings, and there he was content to live until the Lord called him home, in his hundredth year. J.N. Darby wrote,

*This world is a wilderness wide,*
*I have nothing to seek or to choose;*
*I've no thought in the waste to abide;*
*I have nought to regret nor to lose.*

It is not our argument that we ought to emulate the example of these men in every detail, yet one cannot but wonder if the source of their spiritual power and effectiveness lay, in part at least, in their loose hold upon material and temporal things.

Before concluding this section on the use of our money, we must consider in a positive way, how we can *'give to the Lord'*. Both Old and New Testaments present us with helpful examples and principles which we do well to examine carefully. The following points may summarise the biblical teaching: —

1. We should give REGULARLY.

Paul, in 1 Corinthians 16:2, instructs the church at Corinth thus: — "Upon the first day of the week, let every one of you lay by him in store." The habit of regular, weekly giving is one which we should foster.

2. We should give PROPORTIONATELY.

1 Corinthians 16:2 goes on to say, "as God hath prospered him." There is no question of a 'flat-rate' being imposed on every member of the church. The Lord's method leaves the way clear for each to respond in proportion to his or her income.

3. We should give SYSTEMATICALLY.

Orderliness is a good quality in every department of life, and one which we should endeavour to cultivate. In handling our financial matters, let us aim at being methodical, thereby ensuring that all our accounts are settled on time, and that the Lord's portion is "laid by in store."

4. We should give CHEERFULLY.

"God loveth a cheerful giver." (2 Corinthians 9:7) The Greek word 'hilaros', here translated 'cheerful', denotes a readiness of mind and joyousness which make us willing to act. It is the root from which our word 'hilarious' is derived.

5. We should give UNOSTENTATIOUSLY.

In Matthew 6 our Lord spoke against making a display of almsgiving. There is to be no calling of another's attention to what we are giving; indeed, He said, "Let not thy left hand know what thy right hand doeth." (verse 3)

6. We should give WORSHIPFULLY.

Scripture is silent as to how the giving of the saints is to be collected on 'the first day of the week'. In some assemblies, a bag, a basket or a plate is passed around, while in other parts the offering is deposited in a box placed in a convenient position. But whatever method is employed, the material giving of the believers is "an odour of a sweet smell, a sacrifice acceptable, well-pleasing to God." (Philippians 4:18) This lifts it to the level of worship — a tangible evidence of the overflow of each heart, in its appreciation of the wonderful God who has made such giving possible.

The Bible's teaching on stewardship is an intensely practical subject. Properly understood, and sincerely accepted, it will regulate our attitude not only to our money, but also to our time and our 'talents'. (By 'talents' we mean whatever gifts or capabilities the Lord has entrusted to us.) To accept that everything is really His, but is now put into our hands for a little while with a view to being utilized by us for His glory, will bring rich spiritual development into our lives.

As we conclude our study of this subject, reflect upon the following implications of the matter: —

1. Stewardship implies a recognition of the Lord's authority over the Christian's life. It is no longer 'I', 'me' and 'mine' that are the dominant notes in our lives: they are replaced by 'He', 'Him' and 'His.' No longer do we live "unto ourselves", but "unto Him who died and rose again." (2 Corinthians 5:15)

2. Stewardship involves a reinforcement of our sense of accountability to the Lord. Accountability is inextricably interwoven into stewardship; to accept the latter in practical terms, means that we develop a sharp awareness that there will come a day when everything associated with this present life will come under His scrutiny. He will put the final assessment upon it. "We shall all stand before the judgment seat of Christ." (Romans 14:10)

3. Stewardship results in a raising of the level of our attentiveness. To accept sincerely the Bible's teaching on stewardship will produce a carefulness about our use of everything which the Lord has given us. This is not to say that we become tight-fisted and miserly, or incapable of enjoying the good things He has given us. (See 1 Tim. 6:17). But if the over-riding principle — that all is really His — has gripped our hearts, we will be careful lest we squander what does not belong to us! Our Lord defined, 'in Luke 12:42, the kind of steward who gains his master's approval as being "wise" and "faithful". Each of us should strive after these two qualities. Disciplined and thoughtful use of material wealth befits those who aspire to hear the Master's, "Well done", in a future day.

4. Stewardship promotes activity in spiritual matters. Teaching about stewardship is an antidote to idleness. In the 'Parable of the Pounds', ten men heard their lord say, "Occupy till I come". In so saying, he was launching them into activity, and indicating to them that they had only a limited period of time

in which to fulfill his wish. So it is with us! In the light of His imminent coming, let us bestir ourselves to use to the utmost every faculty and possession, for His glory.

*'I've found a Friend! — oh, such a Friend!*
*He bled, He died to save me;*
*And not alone the gift of life,*
*But His own self He gave me.*
*Nought that I have mine own I'll call;*
*I'll hold it for the Giver,*
*My heart, my strength, my life, my all,*
*Are His, and His for ever'.*

James G. Small

# 6. Separation, Commitment and Holiness

### Romans 6:17-23

*17  But God be thanked, that ye were the servants of sin, but ye have obeyed from the heart that form of doctrine which was delivered you.*

*18  Being then made free from sin, ye became the servants of righteousness.*

*19  I speak after the manner of men because of the infirmity of your flesh: for as ye have yielded your members servants to uncleanness and to iniquity unto iniquity; even so now yield your members servants to righteousness unto holiness.*

*20  For when ye were the servants of sin, ye were free from righteousness.*

*21  What fruit had ye then in those things whereof ye are now ashamed? for the end of those things is death.*

*22  But now being made free from sin, and become servants to God, ye have your fruit unto holiness, and the end everlasting life.*

*23  For the wages of sin is death; but the gift of God is eternal life through Jesus Christ our Lord.*

### Romans 12:1,2

*1  I beseech you therefore, brethren, by the mercies of God, that ye present your bodies a living sacrifice, holy, acceptable unto God, which is your reasonable service.*

*2  And be not conformed to this world: but be ye transformed by the renewing of your mind, that ye may prove what is that good, and acceptable, and perfect, will of God.*

The three words which constitute the title of this chapter denote, in general terms, the will of God for all His people. Whatever our role in life, it is God's desire that we should be marked by separation from all known sin, consecration to Him, and wholehearted commitment to His affairs. If these qualities are missing from our every-day living, the effectiveness of our witness for the Lord is seriously impaired. Indeed, if such be the case, we may very well enquire if there is anything to distinguish us from the unconverted amongst whom we live.

As a preliminary, it may be helpful to review the passage above and to be clear in our minds as to what Paul, the writer, is saying. We note that at the beginning, he looks back to his readers' earlier lives, and he gives thanks to God for their CONVERSION. "But God be thanked," he says, "that ye were the servants of sin, but ye have obeyed from the heart that form of doctrine which was delivered you." (verse 17)

We will also observe that he looks at their present situation and urges them to greater CONSECRATION. Thus, in verse 19 he writes, "even so now yield your members servants to righteousness unto holiness."

Coming to the end of the chapter, we can see that Paul projects his mind to the future. He indicates to his readers the final CONSUMMATION of their salvation — "the end everlasting life." (verse 22) It is, of course, true to say that everlasting, or eternal, life is our possession right now, but in this particular case, the apostle is viewing it in its future fulness.

We observe, too, that this section of Romans 6 throws up many contrasts. This is because Paul is thanking God for the wonderful changes that have followed conversion. True conversion is always marked by change! There is a break with the old way of life, and an entering upon a new and different lifestyle. Note how Paul sets "servants of sin" in contrast to "servants of righteousness" (verses 17 and 18). "Iniquity" and "holiness", "death" and "life" are some of the other contrasting terms which he employs in portraying the radical changes effected by God's wonderful grace.

If we look a little more deeply into this passage of Scripture, we shall find that there are three 'word-pictures' lying behind the language which Paul uses. As we focus upon this imagery taken from the first-century world in which Paul lived, and attempt to unravel its spiritual meaning, we shall learn something of the Lord's call to separation, commitment and holiness.

The three 'word-pictures' are these: -
1. A Slave-market.
2. A Moulding, or Casting.
3. An Altar.

## 1. The Slave-market

Throughout the entire paragraph, the word translated as 'servants' (6 times) is 'doulos', which signifies a 'bond-servant' or a 'slave'. Perhaps we need to remind ourselves of what a very powerful institution slavery was in the Roman world. The whole economy of the great Roman Empire depended upon it, and within the iron grip of an often cruel and barbaric system hundreds of thousands of men and women lived out their miserable existence. It is with such a background in his mind that Paul writes to these Christians, reminding them that they once had been "slaves of sin", but now are "slaves of righteousness". (verses 17 and 18)

Imagine, for a moment, the scene in a typical slave-market. Groups of slaves with dejected countenances, stand around. Their heavy chains ensure that there is no chance of escape. Their bodies, perchance, bear evidence of the ill-treatment that has been meted out to them. Owners, both former and prospective, move around, wrangling over prices. Let us suppose that into this depressing scene there comes a kindly, well-disposed man whose heart is moved by a sense of compassion for these miserable, shackled creatures. We watch as he enters into negotiations with a slave owner. In a little while, a price is agreed, the money changes hands and the compassionate man takes his newly acquired 'possession' and leads him away from the market. Stopping, he turns to the slave, and without a word removes his chains. Then, looking into the slave's face, he says, "You are free; you may go!"

"Free?" queries the slave. "You mean I am no longer a slave?"

"Yes," answers his kind benefactor. "You are free, for I have bought you at considerable personal cost, not to impose further suffering upon you, but to give you the freedom of which you have dreamed for so many years!"

What, do you think, would the slave's reaction be? Surely it is not inconceivable that he would turn to his new-found friend, and with deep emotion, say, "Thank you, kind sir, but I am yours, for you have bought me. I have no other will but to serve you, in appreciation of your kindness to me. My greatest freedom, indeed, my supreme joy, lies in whole-hearted, voluntary submission to you, from this day onwards. I cannot, and will not leave you. Your love and kindness have won me completely; take me and let me be your willing slave, all the days of my life!"

A 'word-picture', behind which lies rich spiritual truth! We were 'slaves of sin', but are now 'made free'. Is there, on our part, a readiness to 'yield our members slaves to righteousness', knowing that such a course can only issue in 'everlasting life'?

The imagery of the slave-market enables us to see that the Biblical doctrine of separation has both a negative and a positive aspect. Perhaps, in the past, the negative aspect has been over-emphasised — our thinking has been largely in terms of what we must NOT do and where we must NOT go. We ought, however, to realize that while the Scriptures do stress the importance of 'separation FROM', they maintain a balance by urging us to be 'separate UNTO...' (See e.g., 2 Corinthians 6:14-18, Colossians 3:1,2)

Just as the slave whom we have been visualizing terminated his old life, and surrendered himself willingly to his new owner, so we are to make a clean break with our sinful past and to yield ourselves in unreserved commitment to the One who has purchased us by His own blood. The rest of our lives are to be lived, not unto ourselves, but unto Him who died for us and rose again. (See 2 Corinthians 5:15)

## 2. The Moulding, or Casting

It is an instructive experience to visit a foundry and watch molten metal being poured into a shape which has been made ready for it. The metal, as it cools and hardens, will take on the shape of the mould. In this way castings are prepared for many engineering projects.

This picture lies behind the final clause of verse 17 — "that form of doctrine which was delivered you". The word 'form' is used for a cast or frame into which the liquid metal is poured, and in this verse it is employed metaphorically of the teachings of the Gospel, which give 'shape' to the lives of those who believe its message. The Christians, in this figurative language, are the molten material who are being committed, so to speak, to the 'mould' of Christ's teachings. This understanding of the end of verse 17 is corroborated by both the marginal reading and also by the Revised Version. The former says, "whereto ye were delivered", and the latter, "whereunto ye were delivered". The thought appears to be, not so much that of the Gospel being delivered to the Roman believers, but rather, that of the believers being 'delivered unto' the Gospel and its teachings, in much the same way as a pan of molten metal would be 'delivered unto' a mould. As an alternative to the idea of molten metal, Matthew Henry suggests we may take the imagery of 'wax being cast into the impression of the seal, answering it line by line'. (Commentary. Pg. 566)

As we reflect upon the themes of separation, commitment and holiness, this picture language must be very relevant in helping us to understand that God's plan for our lives is to 'shape' us. It is true that through Christ's great redemptive work at Calvary, we have been 'set free', as we saw in the imagery of the slave-market. But liberty is not licence to do as we please! The teachings of the Gospel, especially in their moral implications, act as a mould by which God, through the indwelling Holy Spirit, desires to produce Christ-like qualities in our characters. Galatians 5 presents similar truth in somewhat different terms; there, it is 'the fruit of the Spirit' which is being cultivated in believers' lives, as they submit themselves to His benign influence.

God's ultimate objective is that we shall all bear the likeness of His Son, our Lord Jesus! "Behold, now are we the children of God, and it is not yet made manifest what we shall be. We know that if he shall be manifested, we shall be like him; for we shall see him even as he is." (1 John 3:2 R.V.) This glorious moment is still ahead of us! In the meantime, we have the privilege of submitting ourselves to the moulding influences of His Word, and thereby taking on, little by little, the 'shape' that His good will has planned for us.

It is an inescapable fact that the Gospel makes high moral demands of all who believe its glad message. Titus 2:11 and 12 tells us that the grace of God instructs us, to the intent that, denying ungodliness and worldly lusts, we should live soberly, righteously and godly in this present world. We must never allow ourselves to lower the high standards of God's word however much levels of morality and righteousness fall in the society in which we live. If we do, our effectiveness as 'salt' and 'light' will be greatly diminished. (Matthew 5:13,14)

### 3. The Altar

This 'word-picture' arises from verse 19, where the word translated 'yielded' and 'yield' is the same as is translated 'present' in Romans 12:1. It is the technical word for presenting Levitical victims and offerings, and so has strong 'altar' overtones.

As Paul writes verse 19, he appears to be very aware of the need to present Divine truth in a manner in which his readers could assimilate. Hence he says, "I speak after the manner of men because of the infirmity of your flesh," which is to say, "I use this human analogy to bring the truth home to your weak nature".

He then proceeds to remind them that at one period of their lives they had laid their members on the altar for uncleanness and for "iniquity unto iniquity". He is clearly referring to their pre-conversion life-style, when their body-members and mental faculties were dedicated to all manner of vice and lawlessness. It was indeed a perilous course upon which they had embarked, for each form of iniquity led only to a more sordid form of evil. The demands of the 'altars of sin' were incessant, and their outcome increasingly disastrous. It was a highway that could only end in eternal death. (See verse 21)

Then he turns to another altar and urges them to "yield their members servants to righteousness unto holiness". This is the altar of the believer's consecration — the worshipful response of hearts that appreciate God's wonderful grace towards them. Each facet of the personality may be 'yielded' or 'presented' on this altar. In so doing, a Christian is progressing in the path-way of right conduct which befits one who has been set apart for God. Everything is in sharp contrast to the earlier way of life. Whereas former behaviour bore witness to lives that were being lived in separation from God, now there is clear evidence of right standing before God, and separation from the sinful practices of the world.

"Yield your members servants to righteousness unto holiness," is the apostle's appeal in verse 19. It is an appeal for the severing of all ties with the old life, and for the presentation of all their faculties to the God who has transformed their lives so radically. No department of a Christian's life is excluded from the Divine claim. In the consecration of Israel's priests, the blood of the sacrificial ram was applied to the priests' ear, thumb and toe; similarly, every member of the believer's body is to be subject to the power of Christ's cross. (See Exodus 29)

The concept of our total commitment to the Lord is further emphasised in Romans 12:1 and 2. Instead of using the word "members" (as in chapter 6), the apostle employs the word "bodies", thereby calling attention to the fact that the Lord has a claim upon the totality of our being. Every member, every capability, every faculty is to be presented as a "living sacrifice, holy, acceptable unto God". Such a response is "our reasonable service". This concluding phrase of verse 1 conveys the idea that such whole-hearted consecration of heart, mind, will, words and actions is "our spiritual worship". (See R.V. Margin.)

As we travel in our thoughts from the slave-market, to the pouring of molten metal into the mould, and then to the altar of sacrifice and worship, we learn valuable lessons about our separation, our commitment and our holiness of life. All those who have had the experience of spiritual conversion have entered upon a new life. "Old things are passed away; behold, all things are become new." (2 Corinthians 5:17) Let us not shy away from the challenging demands of His love and grace. In sincere appreciation of all He has done for us, let us yield ourselves unreservedly to Him.

> *Saviour! Thy dying love*
> *Thou gavest me,*
> *Nor should I aught withhold,*
> *My Lord, from Thee;*
> *In love my soul would bow,*
> *My heart fulfil its vow,*
> *Some offring bring Thee now,*
> *Something for Thee.*

## *James Naismith*

# 1. The Church: What is it?

The devil is very busy! He is at work in all our lives – and our churches, assemblies. He has been active throughout human history from its very beginning – asking the same question as he asked then, *"Has God said?" (Gen. 3.1)*: questioning the word of Almighty God. Over the course of many centuries, he has been attacking God's written word, the Bible. He tried – in vain – to attack the Living Word, the Son of God when He was on earth. Since the Lord's resurrection and ascension, Satan has, from time to time, persistently and successively assailed various great doctrines of the Bible. Dr. H. L. Willmington has stated that *"during the first few centuries of church history, the devil attacked the doctrine of the deity of Christ. Then...he moved against the doctrine of justification by faith...Again, turning in another direction, he lashed out against the inspiration of the Scriptures...Finally, in a desperate effort to corrupt and confuse the work of God (before the coming of the Son of God), Satan has boldly and brazenly declared all-out war upon the very bride of Christ, the church itself. Today one need only scan the horizon of Christendom to discover just how successful Satan has been along these lines. There is a desperate need for the study of and subsequent return to the scriptural teachings of the church."*[1] This need is great even in the assemblies of God's people, and it behooves us to frequently examine and proclaim the basic Biblical teaching on the church: its principles and practices.

The subject of the Church is one of the most important topics of the New Testament. In the Old Testament, we learn about the LORD (Yahweh, Jehovah) and His earthly people, Israel. In the New Testament, the predominant Subjects are Christ and His heavenly people, the Church. The subject of the

Church pervades the New Testament, introduced by the Lord Jesus in the first New Testament book: **Matthew 16.18**, and continuing through the last book, the Revelation. The Church is Christ's special treasure. **"Christ loved the church and gave Himself for it"** *(Eph. 5.25)* and we should be willing to do the same *(1 John 3.16.)*

***WHAT IS THE CHURCH?*** When asked this question, the average person in North America would probably begin by thinking of a building: a building with a steeple, perhaps a cross; where, on Sunday mornings, people can be seen entering and, later, leaving; where hymns are sung and sermons preached. On further consideration, the person may realize that the term 'church' is also used of a 'denomination': for example; the Roman Catholic Church, Presbyterian Church, etc. Strangely enough, the Bible does not refer to these 'churches' in its pages. In the first place, in New Testament times, people did not gather in special buildings for 'church meetings'. We are told about the **homes** in which they gathered: homes like those of Aquila and Priscilla **(Rom.16.3,5; 1 Cor.16.19)**, Nymphas *(Col. 4.15)* and Philemon *(Phile. 2).* It seems that 'church buildings' were unknown till the late second century A.D. Of course, the Church is a building (the Lord said, *"I will* **build** My *church" (Matt. 16.18),* but not of material bricks or stones, but of spiritual, **"living stones"** *(1 Pet. 2.5; Eph. 2.20-22)* – believers in the Lord Jesus Christ. In New Testament times, too, there were no such things as *'denominations'.* There were of course, different 'religions' with buildings appropriate for their meetings: heathen temples, Jewish synagogues, etc.: but the church was not divided into numerous splinters as today. *"According to the 'World Christian Encyclopedia' (1982), there were an estimated 1,900 church denominations at the beginning of the 20th century."* In 1984 there were *"an estimated 22,000"!*

***"I WILL BUILD MY CHURCH"***: **Matthew 16.18**. *"The Law of First Mention"* states that the first occurrence, in the Bible, of a word or subject is an important key to its meaning throughout the Bible. In this verse, the "**Church**" is mentioned for the very first time in the Bible. This is doubly significant here, for the Lord Jesus is the Speaker! His statement is commenced by the five most important words that were ever spoken or written about the church: "**I will build My church**". They are so important that we should consider every one of them individually in order to gain an understanding of what the church is.

*"I": The Person* Who is building the church. The Lord Jesus Christ is the Divine Architect and Builder; He is also the Foundation, the Cornerstone, and the Capstone *(1 Pet. 2.6,7)*; He is also, of course, the Head of the Body *(Eph. 5.23; Col.1.18)*, the Bridegroom of the Bride *(Eph. 5.25)*, the Shepherd of the Flock *(John 10.11,16)*, and the Sovereign Lord in the midst of the Lampstands ("Candlesticks": *Rev.1.13,20; 2.1)*.

*"WILL": a. His Purpose*: to build His church. What a glorious purpose! We certainly know that, since He is God, the Sovereign Lord of the universe, His purpose will never be frustrated. He will fulfil it completely as He has planned.

*b. His Prediction*. He was anticipating the future. Theologians differ in their views of when the church began. Some trace its origin back to Adam and Eve; others to Abraham; others to John the Baptist; etc. The Lord Jesus has settled the question once and for all: it was still future when He spoke these words to His disciples at Caesarea Philippi ("**I** *will* **build**"). Some essential things had to happen before the building could begin. **First**, the Lord Jesus had to die to pay the purchase price *(Eph. 5.25)* and "to *reconcile both (Jews and Gentiles) in one body by the cross (Eph. 2.16)*. **Secondly**, He had to **rise from the dead** to be the living Builder, imparting life to the "dead" stones (Eph. 2.1,5,20), so that they would be "*living stones*" *(1 Pet. 2.5)*. **Thirdly**, He had to **ascend** to heaven to be their Ascended Head at God's right hand (Eph.1.20-23). **Fourthly**, He had to **send the Holy Spirit** *(John 15.26)* to indwell every believer, baptizing them into the body of Christ *(1 Cor.12.13)*. All this was completed when the Spirit descended at Pentecost. Three thousand were added to the disciples, and, thereafter, **the Lord added to the church daily such as should be** (or, *were being)* **saved**" *(Acts 2.1-4,41,47)* We conclude that the church began at Pentecost.

*"BUILD": The Process,* that, for nearly 20 centuries now, has been going on, uninterruptedly, under the sovereign direction of the Master Builder. It is being carried out with infinite skill and omniscient wisdom. The Lord of Glory, Who is engaged in this building, is going to be honoured through it and we, His church, are being blessed.

> *"View the vast building, see it rise;*
> *The work how great! the plan, how wise!*
> *O wondrous fabric! power unknown.*
> *That rests it on the 'Living Stone'".*
>
> – Samuel Medley

*"MY": His Possession.* To Whom does the church belong? Not to any minister, pastor, archbishop or pope, but solely to the Lord Himself! The church universal is His; and every local church also belongs to Him. He is the Head of the church; He is the Lord of every local church, and of every believer who is in the church. We sometimes speak about "our church" or "our assembly"; but, in reality, my assembly does not belong to me: I belong to it and the assembly belongs to the Lord – and so do I! The Lord Jesus is the Owner, the Possessor. He is the Possessor of all things. He is the Possessor of the church!

*"CHURCH": His People.* The word **"church"** is the translation of the Greek *'ekklesia'* (from which are derived words like 'ecclesiastical', 'ecclesiology') which simply means: **"called out"**. As already noted, the **"church"** is not a building of lifeless material stones, nor a dead organization; but is composed of living stones forming a vital organism. At present – and through the centuries since Pentecost – the Holy Spirit has been calling out from among the nations a *"people*

*for His name" (Acts 15.14).* The Lord is still adding to the church daily those who are being saved. All who receive Him as Lord of their lives and Saviour from sin have been called out from the world and brought into the Church that belongs to our blessed Lord. The word *"ekklesia"* is not used of any material building. In *Acts 19.37*, we read *of "robbers of churches"* but the word for churches here is not *"ekklesia":* the phrase, *"robbers of churches",* translates an adjective, which, literally, means "robbing temples". The word "ekklesia" is used *in Acts 7.38* of *"the church in the wilderness",* referring to Israel: this does not mean that the nation of Israel was the church then; but simply that they were *called out* by God from Egypt. The same word is used, on three occasions, *in Acts 19*, of a congregation in uproar *(32,41)* and of a *"lawful assembly"* of citizens *(39)*: in each case, the English (KJV) translation is "**assembly**" – which may well be the best translation of the Greek word wherever it occurs. On all other occasions, the word is used of an assembly of God's people, Christians: sometimes of the universal church; sometimes, of local expressions of the church.

*THE COMMENCEMENT OF THE CHURCH: When did the church begin?* As already noted, the church began at Pentecost; that was its birthday. Through the Acts, we read the story of many chapters being added to the history of the church. Subsequently, until now, many other chapters have been and are being added to this marvellous story. Each chapter concerns others being saved and added to the church.

*THE COMPOSITION OF THE CHURCH: Who are in the church?* As at the beginning, those who were *saved* were added *(Acts 2.47)*, so it is today. Only those who are living stones, having been brought to the Lord Jesus as their Lord and Saviour, and thus *possessing* eternal life through Him, are in His church. One day, perhaps very soon, the last stone will be added to the Building.

*THE COMPLETION OF THE CHURCH: When will the church be completed?* The church will be complete when the last stone will be added. Then, *"the Lord Himself shall descend from heaven ... the dead in Christ shall rise first: Then we who are alive and remain shall be caught up together with them to meet the Lord in the air"* *(1 Thess. 4.16,17).* What a glorious day that will be! Rapturcd to glory! For ever with the Lord! Every "living stone", every saint in the church will hear His shout. *"Praise the Lord! We'll all be there!"*

> *"Upon the golden seashore sand*
> *I wrote my name one day;*
> *The waves came in and when they left,*
> *My name had passed away.*
>
> *Upon the shifting sands of time*
> *Men write their names today,*
> *But when eternal years roll in,*
> *Their names will pass away.*
>
> *Upon the spotless Book of Life,*
> *God wrote my name one day;*
> *Eternal years can never take*
> *That God-penned name away.*
>
> *My name is there for ever*
> *Through all God's endless days;*
> *For He Who died to put it there*
> *Has put it there to stay."*

**"UPON THIS ROCK I WILL BUILD MY CHURCH"**: Strangely enough, there has been much controversy in "Christian" circles about what or who **"this rock"** is. The Lord Jesus prefaced this statement with the words, **"Thou art Peter"**. Since the Greek words for **Peter** *(petros)* and **rock** *(petra)* are very similar, many believe (including, of course, Roman Catholics) that Peter is the rock on which the Lord stated His church was to be built. However, while similar, the two words are different. In the *"Expository Dictionary of New Testament Words"*, W. E. Vine states that *petra* (rock) *"denotes 'a mass of rock' as distinct from petros"* (Peter), which is *"'a detached stone or boulder'; or a stone that might be thrown or easily moved"* [3]. The word *'petra'* (rock) occurs sixteen times

70

in the New Testament: eleven times it refers to a solid mass of rock; four times to the Lord Jesus Christ, the Rock; and one time, here in *Matt.16.18*. It seems clear that the Lord is referring to Himself: *"On Christ the solid Rock we stand."* But there are other good reasons for believing that He was not meaning Peter. What a flimsy foundation if the Rock is Peter! Five verses later, the Lord has to rebuke Peter: *"Get thee behind Me, Satan" (v.23)*. Not very long afterwards, Peter denied his Lord three times, the third time with oaths and curses *(Matt. 26.69-75)*. Then, after his restoration and his great service for the Lord recorded in the first twelve chapters of the Acts, Paul had to withstand him to the face and rebuke him for his hypocrisy *(Gal. 2.11-14)*. He would certainly not have made a solid rock foundation on which to build the church of Christ! The character *of petros* – a movable stone – is a more fitting description of Peter!

Moreover, there are other clear evidences, from both Old and New Testaments, that the Lord is the Rock. Frequently in the Old Testament, especially in the Psalms, the Lord is declared to be **"the Rock"**, **"my Rock"** (e.g. *Ps.18.2,31,46*). This is confirmed in the writings of Paul: **"Other foundation can no man lay than that is laid, which is Jesus Christ"** (*1 Cor. 3.11*). Peter himself declared it in *1 Peter 2.6-8*, where he describes his Lord (not himself)as **"chief corner stone...the head of the corner and a stone of stumbling and a rock of offence."**

> *"On Christ salvation rests secure;*
> *The Rock of Ages must endure;*
> *Nor can that faith be overthrown*
> *Which rests upon the 'Living Stone'*
> *No other hope shall intervene;*
> *To Him we look, on Him we lean;*
> *Other foundations we disown,*
> *And build on Christ, the 'Living Stone'."*
>
> Samuel Medley

**THE GATES OF HELL SHALL NOT PREVAIL AGAINST IT**: This does not mean that the *gates* of hell (Hades) are going to attack the church but not prevail! Gates are not a means of offence but of defence. The Lord Jesus is saying that the Church is going to attack the gates of hell and shall be victorious. The powers of death were overcome by the Lord Himself when He arose triumphant from the grave. Again, at the Rapture, the resurrection of saints who have died, and the rapture of saints who are living will demonstrate the triumph of Christ and His people over the gates of Hades.

*"His be the Victor's name*
*Who fought our fight alone'*
*Triumphant saints no honour claim,*
*Their conquest was His own.*
*By weakness and defeat*
*He won the mead and crown;*
*Trod all our foes beneath His feet*
*By being trodden down.*
*He Satan's power laid low;*
*Made sin, He sin o'erthrew;*
*Bowed to the grave destroyed it so,*
*And death by dying slew."*

Whitlock Grandy

*LOCAL CHURCHES:* Two chapters after the first occurrence of the word, **"church"**, in the Bible *(Matt.16.18)*, the word occurs twice in the same verse, **Matt.18.17**: "**If he** (a brother who has committed a trespass against another) **shall neglect to hear them** (two or three witnesses), **tell it unto the** *church (ekklesia);* **but if he neglect to hear the** *church (ekklesia)*, **let him be unto thee as an heathen man and a publican.**" In His omniscience, the Lord anticipated the building of the church through the centuries following Pentecost, and the problems that would arise between believers in local churches. Soon after Pentecost, it would become impossible, for geographical and numerical reasons, for all the church to meet at one time in one place – until the Rapture, when we shall all be caught up together to meet the Lord in the air. In **Matt.16.18,** the Lord Jesus was speaking about the **church** in its **universal** aspect: **"I will build My**

**church"**. Here, in **Matt.18.17**, He was speaking about a **local church**. Many subsequent references in the New Testament are to the local church. A local church may be defined, very simply, as "*a gathering of believers in Christ in a given locality*": believers who acknowledge Christ as Lord, the Spirit of God as resident in every believer, and the Bible as the inspired word of God, whose principles and practices they acknowledge and obey.

Each local church is a representation – a "model" – in the locality where it is, of the universal church and should be manifesting the characteristics of the universal church. At the end of a meeting in an assembly in a town in Ontario, a brother shook my hand and said: "*You said that each local church is a model of the church universal! Do you know what a model is?*" I replied, "*Yes, I think I do!*" He said, "*Let me tell you a story - of a husband and wife, not long married. The husband took his new wife to meet some of his friends and working companions. Introducing her to them, he said: 'She is a model wife!' Of course, she was very delighted that he thought so much of her and complimented her so highly. But, as she pondered her husband's compliment, she began to have doubts, and, on the next morning, when her husband was at work, she took out a dictionaary, looked up the word, 'model, and discovered the meaning, 'a miniature representation of the real thing'! Her doubts were confirmed! Her husband's remark no longer seemed complimentary!*" But that is what a model is: consider a model train, a model ship, a model of a city being developed, etc. When I was in India, ministering the Word, in 1986, I decided to bring back some souvenirs for my wife and family and some friends. I was taken by a friend to a store in Bangalore, where I purchased for my wife an ivory necklace, with a very small, but beautifully carved "model" of the Taj Mahal, the world-famous, magnificent building in Agra, North India. On a subsequent visit to India in 1994, we visited the Taj Mahal and were delighted to discover how good a replica was the model on my wife's necklace. In the same way, each local church should be a representation in that locality of the universal church.

At the moment of our conversion, each one of us was added by the Lord to the church universal. We have all a responsibility, if we are genuine believers, to seek, as Saul of Tarsus did *(Acts 9.26)*, to "join" ourselves to the disciples in our locality, to enter into fellowship with other believers in a local church, to share the privileges, fulfil the responsibilities and carry out the practices of a local church.

1. Willmington, H.L.: "Guide to the Bible", (Tyndale House Publishers, Inc., Wheaton, Illinois,1981), p.691.
2. Omanson, R.L.: "Evangelical Dictionary of Theology", Walter A. Elwell, (Baker Book House, Grand Rapids, Michigan,1984), p.231.
3. Vine, W.E.: "Expository Dictionary of Biblical Words", (Thomas Nelson Publishers, Nashville; Camden; New York;1985), "Rock", p.537.

# 2. Evangelism

In the early days of the "brethren movement", godly brethren placed great emphasis on evangelism. They had a commitment to spreading the Gospel both near and far. By their efforts, individually and collectively, thousands were brought into saving contact with the Lord Jesus Christ. Wherever they preached, souls were saved. The rapid expansion of their numbers was due in part to their Christlikeness and unworldliness, but, in a large measure, to their Gospel outreach. In the years following those early days, it has been a characteristic and a principle of the assemblies of God's people to proclaim the Gospel of the grace of God, in the area surrounding each assembly, and *"unto the uttermost parts of the earth"*, in accordance with our Lord's command *(Acts 1.8)*. Since Anthony Norris Groves, the first "brethren" missionary left Britain for Baghdad in 1829, many thousands of assembly missionaries have gone from different countries of the world to serve the Lord in foreign lands. That this work is still going on, to the glory of God, is evident from the CMML Missionary Prayer Handbook and Missions Magazine; and the British "Echoes" Daily Prayer Guide and Missionary Magazine, and corresponding Handbooks and Magazines from other countries. It would be good if every assembly believer read such lists and reports daily and prayed for the Lord's work going on throughout the world.

*Evangelism* has been defined as *"one beggar telling another beggar where to find bread"!* We are surrounded, in our world, by multitudes of spiritual "beggars": men, women, and children starving spiritually. They may be rich in material resources and physical benefits, but spiritually, they are beggars. We, believers, have found the **"Bread of Life"**, Who alone can satisfy the deepest needs of mankind. We have the unspeakable privilege and awesome responsibility of dispens-

75

ing that satisfying Bread, by proclaiming Christ, **"the living Bread"** *(John 6.48,51)*, and presenting Him to them for their acceptance as Lord and Saviour.

In the ninth century B.C., four lepers (*2 Kings 7*) were sitting in the gate of the city of Samaria, capital of the northern kingdom of Israel. The city was under siege by the Syrian armies, and the citizens were in desperate plight. They were without the sustenance of life and needed bread. So serious was their situation that some had even resorted to cannibalism to satisfy their hunger. The lepers in the gate, of course, shared their plight. They had a consultation with one another and reasoned: *"Why do we stay here until we die?"* One alternative was to go into the city, but the famine was there; the people there were in the same extremity and had no food for themselves, much less for any visitors! Then they thought about going into the camp of the besieging armies of Syria: the worst that could happen was that they would be killed and die there: but there was the glimmer of possibility that the Syrians might save them alive. So off they set in the twilight to go to the Syrian camp. Surprise! Surprise! No one was there! The Syrians had left, having heard a noise – that God initiated – of chariots, horses and *"of a great host"*. Concluding that the king of Israel had hired other armies to attack them, the Syrians had fled, leaving everything behind them. The four lepers had the time of their lives, going from tent to tent, eating and drinking and plundering the precious possessions that were left behind. Then they stopped and had another consultation. **"We do not well"**, they said, **"this is a day of good tidings and we hold our peace!"** Off they went, back to the city to tell to their "fellow beggars" where they could find bread. Like these lepers, we have found *the* **Source** of bread: the Bread of eternal life. We have good tidings to tell to the starving multitudes, yet so many of us 'hold our peace'!

Another definition of **Evangelism** is *"Love with flesh on"*. Believers are frequently exhorted to "love one another", but we should also love those who are outside the fold of God's grace. Just as **"God so loved the world that He gave His only begotten Son"**, so we have a responsibility to give ourselves in love for others, to clothe our love in human flesh, to bring the love of God, through our hearts and lives, to the people we contact daily.

A good definition of **Evangelism** used years ago by the Presbyterian Church of the U.S.A. reads: *"Evangelism is so to present Jesus Christ, in the power of the Holy Spirit, that men shall come to put their trust in God through Him, to accept Him as their Saviour from the guilt and power of sin, to serve Him as Lord in the fellowship of the Church and to follow Him in the vocations of the common life."* This is the responsibility of every believer in the Lord Jesus Christ, and of all our assemblies.

The word, **"evangelism"**, does not occur in the King James Version of the Bible, although the Greek words, from which it is derived, occur quite frequently. For example, *euangelion,* (literally, good news) is translated "**Gospel**"; and *euangelizo,* "**declare glad tidings**", "**preach the Gospel**". The word, "**evangelist**" occurs three times in the New Testament: ***Eph. 4.11,12:*** **"And He** (the ascended Lord) **gave some, apostles; and some, prophets; and some, *evangelists;* and some, pastors and teachers; for the perfecting of the saints, for the work of the ministry, for the edifying of the body of Christ."** The first two of these gifts were 'foundation gifts': *"Ye are...built upon the foundation of apostles and prophets"* (*Eph. 2.19,20*), and were not given after the foundation was laid in New Testament times. Immediately after these foundation gifts is the gift of **evangelist**. Using this text, Mr. Montague Goodman, began his chapter on *"Evangelists and Evangelism"* in a *Symposium* on *"The Church"*, with the sentence: *"By far and away the most important function of the churches is to evangelize the world".* *He* continued, *"Is it not significant that in the enumeration of the special gifts with which Christ endowed His Church through the Spirit, first and foremost (after the foundation gifts of apostle and prophet) should be named the evange-*

*list?... The pastors and teachers so prominent in organized Christianity today are subordinate in order of precedence to the far less esteemed evangelist. And truly his ministry is by far the most vital to the world and, indeed, to the life and growth of the Church itself.* "[1]

**Acts 21.8:** Philip was one of seven appointed to "serve tables" *(Acts 6.1-6)*, a task sometimes associated with deacon service. In Acts 8, we discover why he was called *"evangelist"*; he is a specific example of such a gift to the church. In verse 5, we read that **"Philip went down to the city of Samaria, and *preached* Christ unto them"**; and the people gave heed to his preaching *(v.6)* and **"believed Philip preaching the things concerning the kingdom of God and the name of Jesus Christ and were baptized"** *(v.12)*. Later, guided by **"the angel of the Lord"** *(v.26)*, Philip moved from a city with many people, to a desert where he led one man to Christ, the Ethiopian eunuch. From the Scriptures the Ethiopian was reading (Is. 53), **"Philip *preached* unto him Jesus"**, resulting in his salvation and baptism (vv.35-38). That is **evangelism**! Preaching Christ! Preaching Jesus! To the crowds in the city! To the individual in the desert! Our task in evangelism is not so much to talk about ourselves – except to indicate how much the Lord has done for us, but to preach Christ Jesus!

**2 Tim. 4.5:** It is evident, from the two epistles to Timothy that he was a pastor (shepherd) and a teacher. The apostle Paul, in these epistles, encouraged him in his pastoral and teaching ministry. In the last chapter, he exhorted Timothy to **"do the work of an *evangelist*"**. Timothy may also have had the gift of an evangelist, but he was primarily a pastor and teacher. So it is with us: whether or not we have *the gift of evangelist,* we do have the responsibility to do *the work of an evangelist.* As we have seen from the example of Philip, evangelism can be public or private; to the multitude or the individual. We may not be able to preach the Gospel from a public platform, but we should all seize opportunities to speak individually to those whom we contact daily.

*"If you cannot speak like angels,*
*If you cannot preach like Paul,*
*You can tell the love of Jesus,*
*You can say He died for all."*

**EVANGELISM IN THE CHURCH:** The New Testament contains several very instructive illustrations of the church: for example, a building, body, bride, flock, etc. The illustration the Lord used of the seven churches in Asia in the first three chapters of Revelation is **"lampstands"** *(Rev.1.12,13,20; 2.1;* mistranslated *"candlesticks"* in the K.J.V.), whose function is to shine as lights in a dark world *(Phil. 2.15)* and to bear witness to our ascended Lord and Redeemer. Every church is also like "a **city**...set on a hill" *(Matt. 5.14)*, shining its light on those around. At Sychar, the Lord Jesus used another metaphor to emphasize the necessity to evangelize. *"Lift up your eyes, and look on the fields; for they are white already to harvest" (John 4.35)*. As reapers in the harvest-field of the world, we should not only lift up our *eyes* to see the needs around us, but also our *voices* – in prayer to the *Master*, the Lord of the harvest *(Matt. 9.38)*, and in proclamation of the Gospel to the *multitude*.

The Lord's last commands to His disciples prior to His ascension are challenging for us today. Matthew recorded this command: **"Go ye therefore, and make disciples** ('teach', K.J.V.) **of all nations, baptizing them in the name of the Father, and of the Son, and of the Holy Ghost, teaching them to observe all things whatsoever I have commanded you: and, lo, I am with you alway, even unto the end of the world** (age)" *(28.19,20)*. **Mark** put it this way: **"Go ye into all the world, and preach the Gospel to every creature"** *(16.15)*. **Luke** wrote, in the *Gospel,* **"Repentance and remission of sins should be preached in His name among all nations, beginning at Jerusalem"** *(24.47)*; and, in the *Acts*, again quoting the words of the Lord, **"Ye shall receive power, after that the Holy Ghost is come upon you: and ye shall be witnesses unto Me both in Jerusalem, and in all Judaea, and in Samaria, and unto the uttermost part of the earth"**

(*1.8*). What an emphasis our Lord placed on evangelism in His last commands and instructions to His disciples: surely intended for His people through the centuries till His return! Dare we disappoint Him? How we have failed Him – and more so as the day of His return draws near! He is still looking for obedient servants and faithful witnesses to herald His name, His work, and His blessings to those around us who have not yet heard of Him, and for whom He shed His precious blood.

**METHODS OF EVANGELISM BY THE LOCAL CHURCH**: First of all, every person in church fellowship has a responsibility to engage in **personal evangelism**, winning souls for Christ by the testimony of our lives and lips, and by bringing them to a place where they can hear the Gospel being proclaimed. In addition to this, there is a variety of methods that can and should be used, where appropriate, by the local church to reach the lost for Christ:

*1. Children's and Youth Programs:* What a wonderful outreach this is, with great opportunities to reach into the hearts and homes of children when they can most easily be won for the Lord! Sunday Schools seem to have fallen upon evil times in many places. In many assemblies, those attending are mostly from the homes of believers. Parents used to bring their children; now they don't even send them! Sometimes, they don't even let them go! But many children can be attracted to other children's activities: week-night meetings, Awana programs, children's clubs; camps etc..

*2. Ladies' Activities:* in many cases, the main outreach, at least to adults. They are given different names: *"Coffee-hours"*, *"Time-out"*, *"Oasis"*, etc.; usually with attractive demonstrations, travelogues, crafts, and other programs, in addition to a Gospel message.

*3. Men's Programs:* presentation of a topic of interest, followed by a proclamation of the Gospel of Jesus Christ.

*4. Neighbourhood Evangelism:* including neighbourhood Bible studies in homes of believers or their neighbors; door-to-door distribution of tracts, booklets, or even New Testaments or Bibles, with invitations to special church activities; arranging of activities – trips, hikes, special events – in which the neighbors can join with the believers; etc.

*5. Radio and Television Evangelism:* It is becoming increasingly difficult to obtain prime listening and viewing time in most places. The Family Bible Hour, broadcast from St. Catharines, Ontario, has an excellent and well-received program, presenting the Gospel in a clear and interesting manner and has been used around the world, in many different languages. Assemblies can purchase air time on their local radio stations and can use the program to announce local church services: a very worthwhile investment!

*6. Hospitals and Homes for Seniors etc.:* What an important avenue to reach people in critical stages of health, or nearing the end of life's journey! While aiming to reach the young for Christ, we should not forget the senior citizens who are about to embark on the journey to eternity.

*7. Prison Ministries:* a very significant sphere of evangelistic ministry: to persons who, because of their crimes, may, at least in some cases, be amenable to the Gospel proclamation of forgiveness of sins through faith in Christ. Emmaus courses are being widely and effectively used in this form of evangelism – and in discipling new believers.

*8. Open Air Services: "No better vault can be found than that which has the sky for its ceiling. No better place than the market square, public park, or equivalent of a Mars' Hill" (E. W Rogers).* It is not always easy to obtain permission to preach in the open air, because of complaints from citizens or pleasure seekers that their peace is being disturbed. It is, however, a very valuable means of outreach if permission is granted. Most of the Lord's preaching and teaching was done in the open air: also the preaching of John the Baptist. Paul, the Apostle used it, e.g. at Athens, although he often used synagogues to preach the Gospel. Care should be taken in choosing those who have the gift of evangelism and can present the Gospel clearly: it may be the only opportunity some listeners have of hearing the good news of God's salvation in Christ.

*9. Regular Gospel Meetings* seem, sadly, to have a diminishing role in assemblies, and to be a thing of the past in some. The writer has been told on several occasions by members of the audience after a Family Bible Hour or Gospel meeting that "the Gospel hasn't been preached here like that for a long time!"

There are those in assembly fellowship who assert that the assembly is not the place to preach the Gospel! They claim that there is no example of Gospel preaching in the New Testament churches! They use *Acts 2.42* as a proof text: *"They continued stedfastly in the apostles' doctrine and fellowship, and in breaking of bread, and in prayers"* – with no mention of evangelism! But note the last verse *(47)* of the chapter: *"The Lord added to the church daily such as should be* (or, *were being) saved".* How were they saved? By the believers presenting the Gospel to them!

***The Church at Antioch*** might be described as a **"Model New Testament Church"**: it became *"the metropolis of Gentile Christianity"* and the centre for worldwide missionary activity in the first century. In **Acts 11.19-30**, we read of the beginnings and progress of the church there. How did it begin? By the preaching of the Gospel: "They who were scattered abroad...travelled as far as....Antioch **preaching the word to none but Jews only... and when they were come to Antioch, spake unto the Grecians,** *preaching the Lord* **Jesus"** (11.19,20). Note the two words for **"preach"**: the first, in **v.19**, *"preaching* the word"*, is simply *'speaking',* the same word translated *"tell"* in *v.14* and *"speak"* in *v.15*. This was personal evangelism, *'gossiping the Gospel'.* The second word, in **v.20**: *"preaching* the Lord Jesus"**, means *'proclaiming the Gospel'.* Note also the two topics: really two in one, *a.* **"The Word"** of God; b. **"The Lord Jesus"**, the Centre of the Gospel message and of thc Word of God. These are the essentials of evangelism: preaching *the Word* and *the Lord.* These were the subjects of all the preaching in Acts, as seen in all the recorded sermons. Note the progress of the church: **"Much people was added unto the Lord" (v.24)**. Evidently, the Gospel preaching continued, even after the church was established. Indeed, it was the church that was preaching the Gospel. Note the further progress in **Acts 13.1-4**. The **evangelistic church** has now become the **missionary church**, sending two of their leading teachers and preachers as missionaries to the *"regions beyond" (2 Cor.10.16)*. Their evangelism started at home and continued throughout the Roman empire. So today, each assembly has responsibility to the immediate neighborhood, *and* to the mission-field.

*Other New Testament Churches*: The New Testament epistles demonstrate the same activity of each assembly in evangelism, for example:

**The Church in Thessalonica**. *1 Thessalonians,* probably the first church epistle, records how the Gospel came to the Thessalonians (1.5 ... 8) – how it started; then how it continued: "From you (church of the Thessalonians) **sounded out the Word of the Lord**".

**The Church in Philippi**, one of the last church epistles, written near the end of Paul's ministry. He wrote about their service in *2.15,16*: "**Ye shine as lights in the world**" – the witness of their *lives*; "**holding forth the word of life**" – the witness of their *lips*.

**The Church at Corinth**: *1 Cor. 1.17 – 2.5.* In an epistle that highlights church principles and practices, the apostle begins, in the first chapter, by emphasizing the importance of preaching the Gospel. Note the frequent references to "preaching": five Greek words are used for "preaching" and "declaring" the Gospel in these verses.

*Why Should we Preach the Gospel in the Assemblies?* Here are 6 reasons:

*1*. **The Emphasis on preaching in the Bible**: the prophets of the Old Testament; and, in the New Testament: John the Baptist, the Lord Jesus, Peter and Paul all preached God's message to men's hearing and hearts.

*2*. **The Gospel is God's Good News for Man,** whether ancient man or "modern man"! It has been preached for close to 20 centuries and has never lost its power: it is *"the power of God unto salvation" (Rom.1.16).* Man needs it as much as ever. It is the only message that can solve man's deepest problem – sin; and provide shelter from coming judgment.

*3.* **One of the Lord's last commands on earth** was to preach the Gospel – as already stated.

*4.* **The Gospel sounds God's warning to the lost and perishing,** and the church has a solemn obligation to issue that warning by preaching the Gospel. God has entrusted it to us as He did to Ezekiel: **"Son of man, I have made thee a watchman unto the house of Israel: therefore hear the word at My mouth, and give them warning from Me" (3.17).**

*5.* **The Gospel is a life-transforming message:** Christ saves souls – and changes lives!

*6.* **The preaching of the Gospel has Side Benefits:** Believers are stirred by it: it brings us joy to hear it proclaimed in simplicity and power. As the Gospel is preached faithfully and clearly, believers learn its fundamental truths and are encouraged and enabled to pass it on more intelligently. A Gospel service should be a guide and aid to personal evangelism.

*THE EVANGEL: WHAT IS THE GOSPEL MESSAGE?* The Acts of the apostles contains several Gospel messages, by Peter, Stephen and Paul, which should be studied carefully to learn the *methods* used in preaching the Gospel and the subject-*matter* to be presented:

*1. Their Messages were Scripturally based:* note especially Peter's sermon at Pentecost, **Acts 2.14-40**, and Paul's at Antioch in Pisidia: **Acts 13.16-41.** If an objection is raised concerning Paul's address at Athens (**Acts 17.22-31**), it should be noted that, while Paul did not quote from the Old Testament to this audience not acquainted with the Scriptures, he did base his message on Old Testament teaching about God and Christ.

*2. Their Preaching was Christ-centred:* in particular, they highlighted in their sermons the death of the Lord Jesus and His glorious resurrection. So should we!

*3. They Emphasized Sin and Judgment*: an emphasis that has disappeared from many evangelical (even assembly) pulpits and platforms. Indeed, there are some leading evangelicals who downplay the subject of hell, asserting that a God of love will not punish sinners in the Lake of Fire. That is contrary to apostolic and Scriptural teaching!

*4. They Preached "Repentance toward God and Faith toward our Lord Jesus Christ"* (**Acts 20.21**): a Gospel message without repentance lacks a vitally important ingredient!

5. **The Introductions to their Messages were based on the circumstances** in which the messages were given and the audience to whom they were presented.

6. **They Concluded their Messages with an Appeal to the audience to turn from their sin** (repentance) **and receive Christ** (faith): *See Acts 2.38; 13.38-41; 17.30,31.*

7. **Their Presentation of the Gospel was Clear and Straightforward**: with no fancy frills to make the message more attractive *('seeker sensitive'),* but clouding or diluting the truth of the word of God. At the end of the 20th century, some *"evangelists"* seem to need more modern methods: increasing use of gimmicks, worldly entertainment and modern marketing schemes: all to make the "Gospel" more 'user friendly' and to attract larger audiences and require bigger church buildings.[2] The exhortation of Paul to Timothy in his last recorded letter is important and appropriate for today: **"Preach the Word"**! *(2 Tim. 4.2).*

1. Goodman, Montague: "Evangelists and Evangelism" in "The Church: A Symposium, edited by J.B.Watson, (Pickering & Inglis, Ltd., London, England,1949), pp.139,140.
2. See: MacArthur, John F., Jr.: "Ashamed of the Gospel", (Crossway Books, Wheaton, Illinois,1993).

# 3. Baptism

From the earliest days of the "brethren movement", emphasis was placed on the two **"ordinances"** given by the Lord to His disciples before He left them. They are part of the Heritage which has been handed down to us, which we should treasure and seek to maintain and pass on to others. Of course, they have been delivered to us, not by the "brethren", but by the Lord Himself. We discover them, as did the early "brethren", in the pages of the word of God , containing the words spoken by the Lord Jesus to His disciples, commanding them to observe these ordinances: the Lord's Supper and Baptism.

These two ordinances have several things in common: *First,* they were both commanded by the Lord and are, therefore, obligatory for His disciples. This is implicit in the word, "ordinances", which may be defined as **"an outward, visible, symbolic act, commanded by Christ and so requiring the obedience of all His people"**. *Second*, both baptism and the Lord's Supper are symbolic. In Baptism, **water** is the symbol – of the grave in which the Lord Jesus was buried: **"we are buried with Him by baptism" (Rom. 6.4).** In the Lord's Supper, the **bread** symbolizes the body of Christ, given on Calvary; and the **cup**, His blood shed for us there. *Third,* both are symbols of the **death** of our Lord for us. *Fourth*, they are both only for believers. *Fifth*, neither is essential for salvation, but both are essential for obedience. *Sixth*, both are presented to us and can be studied in three sections of the New Testament: the **Gospels** describe their **Institution** by the Lord; the **Acts**, the **Illustration** of their observance by the early church; and the **Epistles**, the **Instruction** given about them by the Holy Spirit.

There are also contrasts between the two ordinances: *First,* the Lord's Supper is observed frequently, usually, in assemblies, weekly; baptism only once, after conversion. *Second,* all partake of the Lord's Supper, whereas only the baptized person participates in baptism; others observe. *Third*, while both relate to the death of Christ, the Lord's Supper is a remembrance or commemoration of Christ's death whereas baptism is a public confession of Christ and an identification with Him in His death, burial and resurrection. *Fourth*, at the Lord's Supper, we acknowledge that **Christ died for us, His death for sin**; in baptism, we express, by our action, that **we died with Christ: our death to sin.**

It was the English author and poet, and Nobel prize-winner, Rudyard Kipling, who wrote:

> *"I keep six honest, serving men;*
> *They taught me all I know;*
> *Their names are Who and What and*
> *When and Where and Why* and *How"*.

If we wish to learn about any subject or event – or whatever – it is helpful to ask such questions as: Who did it? Where did it happen? Why did he do it? etc. We can apply such questions frequently in our study of the Bible. For example, when studying an epistle, we should ask, *"Who wrote it? To whom was it written? Where and when was it written? Why was it written? What does it teach?"* We can study the parables similarly. In the same way, we can learn more about baptism by asking the folowing questions:

*WHO SHOULD BE BAPTIZED? THE CANDIDATES.* In Christendom, there are different answers to this question: e.g. believers, children, households. We can find the Scriptural answer to this and the other questions in the three sections of the New Testament mentioned:

1. *The Gospels*: **Matthew 28.19. "Go ye therefore and teach all nations, baptizing them..."** It is important to know that the Greek word translated **"teach"** is different from the word translated **"teaching"** in **v.20.** Whereas in **v.20, "teaching"** means **"instructing,** in **v.19,** the word translated **"teach"** means to disciple, or make disciples of all nations. **"Baptizing them"** does not, of course, mean baptizing all nations – that

would be exceedingly difficult! – but it means baptizing the disciples made by preaching the Gospel to them, so that they believe and become disciples. The Lord here clearly answered the question "Who?" – He meant **"believers"**. Similarly, **Mark** reports (**16.16**): **"He that believeth and is baptized shall be saved"**, again indicating that baptism is for believers; so it is called **"believers' baptism"**.

2. *The Acts*: Many passages in this book about the early Christians and church confirm that their practice was believers' baptism, in accordance with the Lord's command. For example, **Acts 2.38,41**: **"Repent and be baptized every one of you in the name of Jesus Christ ...Then they that gladly received his word were baptized".** Note the order: repentance, faith, baptism: *"repentance toward God, and faith toward our Lord Jesus Christ' (Acts 20.21)*, followed by baptism. Other passages that are equally convincing are 8.12,13, 36,37 (Verse 37 – Philip's statement, *"If thou believest with all thine heart, thou mayest"*, and the eunuch's reply, *"I believe that Jesus Christ is the Son of God"* – is not found in 'the best manuscripts' and may have been a later addition; if so, its very addition indicates the belief and practice of the early Christians; and it is, of course, in agreement with the rest of the New Testament); *16.14,15; 33,34*.

3. *The Epistles:* Baptism is mentioned in five of Paul's epistles and in 1 Peter.

**Rom.6.3,4**: **"Know ye not, that so many of us as were baptized into Jesus Christ were baptized into His death? Therefore we are buried with Him by baptism into death: that like as Christ was raised up from the dead by the glory of the Father, even so we also should walk in newness of life."** This passage does not directly state that believers only – not infants – should be baptized, but it teaches the significance of baptism, and only believers could appreciate this meaning. Certainly, it would be meaningless to infants! Infant baptism cannot be found anywhere in the New Testament: always believers' baptism.

*What about Baptism of Households?* Most of the early "brethren" were convinced that the Scriptures taught believers' baptism, including: *Anthony Norris Groves, George Muller, Henry Craik, Robert C. Chapman, William Kelly.* There was, however, one outstanding exception: *John Nelson Darby*, who wrote: *"I am deeply convinced that a Christian handles evilly if he does not baptize his children."*[1] His stand on infant baptism has been called *"the grave-clothes he brought from the church of Ireland"*. This stand is still taken by some "exclusive brethren".

It is true that the New Testament specifically mentions three households who were baptized:

*1.* **The Household of Lydia: Acts 16.14,15.** We are not told whether Lydia was a married woman with children in her household, so it certainly cannot be asserted that this was a case of "household baptism" and not "believers' baptism". Such evidence as we have points in the opposite direction. Lydia was a **"seller of purple, of the city of Thyatira"**. Years later, the Lord wrote a letter to the church there: see *Rev. 2.18-29.* Did Lydia return home as a believer, win converts and be the means, under God, of planting the church there? We do not know, but it is an interesting speculation! Thyatira was noted for its expensive purple dye which was plentiful there. It seems very likely that Lydia was a business lady, selling purple from her home town across the Aegean Sea in Asia Minor. No mention is made of her husband or family and it is highly probable that her "household" consisted of her assistants in business, who also had become believers.

*2.* **The Household of the Philippian Jailor: Acts 16.33,34.** **"He...was baptized, *he* and all *his*".** There is no doubt in this case, that it was believers' baptism, for **v.34** states that **"he...rejoiced believing in God with *all his house*."** All in the jailor's household were believers!

*3.* **The Household of Stephanas: 1 Cor. 1.16.** **"I baptized also the household of Stephanas"**. Is this simply a case of "household baptism"? No! In the wisdom of God, we do know something else about this household. In **1 Cor. 16.15**, we read,

"The house of Stephanas...is the firstfruits of Achaia, and...they have addicted (devoted) themselves to the ministry (service) of the saints". It is evident that they too were true believers!

*WHEN SHOULD BELIEVERS BE BAPTIZED?* How long after conversion? The Bible does not indicate what period, if any, should elapse. In the examples recorded in the **Acts**, it evidently took place very shortly – if not immediately – after faith in Christ. The Ethiopian eunuch, for example, was baptized before he continued his journey back to Ethiopia (**8.36-39**); and the Philippian jailor at **"the same hour of the night"** when he believed (**16.33**). Evidently, the truth of baptism was presented along with the Gospel message. The practice in most assemblies is to wait until there is evidence of genuine faith in the Lord Jesus Christ. There is often good reason for such delays, but perhaps we should more frequently take the opportunity of baptizing believers sooner after conversion.

*HOW SHOULD BELIEVERS BE BAPTIZED? THE MODE OF BAPTISM.* Should it be done by immersion, sprinkling or affusion (pouring)? The words, pouring and sprinkling, are never used in the New Testament in relation to baptism. The first record of the use of sprinkling for baptism was about A.D. 250 when Novatian lay sick in bed and thought he was going to die. He had water poured all over him on the bed as an act of baptism *(Willmington [2])* There is very good Scriptural evidence that the mode of baptism in New Testament times was by immersion. Consider three lines of evidence:

*1.* **The Meaning of "Baptism".** The word **"baptize"** is transliterated directly from the Greek, *baptizo,* which *"was used among the Greeks to signify the dyeing of a garment, or the drawing of water by dipping a vessel into another"* and *"consists of the processes of immersion, submersion and emergence" (Vine [3])* Dr. H. L. Willmington quotes *Dr. Gordon G. Johnson* in pointing out that three leading Greek Lexicons – by *Liddell and Scott* (Church of England), *Thayer* (Congregational Church) and *Cremer* (German Lutheran) *"agree that the word in its origin means to dip, immerse, submerge or* *overwhelm".* He continues by quoting *Dr. Thomas J. Conant* who, *"in his 'Meaning and Use of Baptizein', sums up a study of the use of the word throughout the history of Greek literature with these words, 'In all, the word has retained its ground meaning without change. From the earliest age of Greek literature down to its close, a period of about 2000 years, not an example has been found in which the word has any other meaning.'"* [4]

2. **New Testament Practice.** When the Lord Jesus was baptized, He **"went up straightway out of the water" (Matt. 3.16)**, indicating that He had already gone down into it. In the baptism of the Ethiopian eunuch, **"they went down both into the water, both Philip and the eunuch; and he baptized him. And when they were come up out of the water, the Spirit of the Lord caught away Philip" (Acts 8.38,39).** There can be no doubt that this was baptism by immersion!

3. **Significance of the Ordinance.** The meaning of baptism, as already indicated, is explained in **Rom. 6.4: "We are buried with Him by baptism into death: that like as Christ was raised up from the dead by the glory of the Father, even so we also should walk in newness of life."** This symbolism can only be expressed by immersion, submersion, (**"buried"**) and emergence (**"raised up again"**).

*WHY SHOULD A BELIEVER BE BAPTIZED?*
*THE REASONS FOR BAPTISM.*

*a.* Every believer should be baptized **because the Lord commanded it** *(Matt.28.19; Mark 16.16).* If there were no other reason, or if we could not understand the basis for the Lord's command, this should be sufficient for every Christian who acknowledges Jesus Christ as Lord.

*b.* The early Christians practised it, as indicated so frequently in the Acts. They have given us a pattern that we should follow. Professor *F.F. Bruce* writes, *"The idea of an unbaptized Christian is simply not entertained in NT."* [5]

*c.* **The Spirit of God has given instructions on baptism** in the epistles of the New Testament (*Rom. 6.3, 4; Col.2.12;*

*1 Pet.3.20,21*). Since He is our divine indwelling Companion, we should surely follow His instructions!

## WHAT IS THE SIGNIFICANCE OF BAPTISM?

*1*. **Baptism is an act of submission and obedience to the Lord Jesus Christ**. By being baptized, we demonstrate that He is our Lord. We can be saved and go to heaven without being baptized but we cannot be truly obedient to our Lord if we refuse baptism.

*2*. **Baptism is a public confession of our faith in Jesus Christ as Lord**. This was certainly true in **Acts 2.38,41**. The 3000 believers repented, acknowledging and renouncing their sin; and they were baptized as a public demonstration of their repentance and faith in the One Whom they had joined in crucifying (**vv. 23,36**). In many cases of baptism, unsaved relatives and friends are invited to witness this act of confession. In many countries of the world, converts from a heathen religion to Christ may be ostracized by their family and friends and sometimes excluded from their homes, when they confess their faith by being baptized.

*3*. **Baptism is an expression of our identification with Christ**. When He died, not only did He die for us, but we died with Him. In baptism, we symbolically demonstrate that we have died and been buried with Him; coming out of the water, we show that we have risen with Him – and should **"walk in newness of life"** (**Rom.6.3,4**), that is, our life is changed and we live a new kind of life on the basis of and in the power of the resurrection of our Lord. Years ago, a Brahmin believer was baptized in the Meeting-room, Broadway, Madras, India. He came to the ceremony wearing, as all Brahmins do, the *'Yagnopavita'* (sacred thread), hanging round his neck. Immediately after his baptism, as he came out of the water, he snapped the thread and threw it into the water, thereby signifying that the old life as a Brahmin had come to an end and that he would thenceforth 'walk in newness of life' in Christ. [6]

*4.* Baptism is the "**answer** ('pledge', NIV) **of a good conscience toward God**" (**1 Pet. 3**.21), that is, a commitment by the person baptized to maintain a good conscience, and express in life what is symbolized in baptism.

*UNSCRIPTURAL VIEWS ABOUT BAPTISM:* Just as there are unscriptural beliefs regarding the persons who should be baptized (infants, households), and the modes of baptism (pouring, sprinkling), so there are false views about what baptism is and does for the person who is baptized:

*l. Baptismal Regeneration*: In many "churches", it is believed and stated at the baptism that, when a person – usually an infant or child – is baptized, he or she becomes *"a child of God and an inheritor of the kingdom"*. This is, of course, quite contrary to Biblical teaching: (a) *about baptism.* The Scriptures never state or imply that baptism is a means of regeneration or salvation (The Lord's words in *Mark 16.16* are discussed in the next section); and (b) *about regeneration.* The Scriptures frequently state and make clear that new birth and salvation are only by faith in the Lord Jesus Christ: for example, "**As many as** *received Him*, **to them gave He power to become the sons of God, even to them that** *believe on His name*" (**John 1.12**). "**That whosoever** *believeth in Him* **should…***have everlasting life*" (**John 3.16**). "*Believe in the Lord Jesus Christ* **and thou shalt be saved**" (**Acts 16.31**).

*2. Baptism: Essential to Salvation?* There are certain groups of "Christians", who, while rejecting baptismal regeneration – baptism as the means of eternal life – assert that it is essential for salvation – in addition to faith in Christ. Now, baptism is essential – for obedience to the Lord, but not for salvation. Persons who put their trust in the Lord Jesus are saved before they are baptized, and, if they die before being baptized, they will assuredly go to heaven. The repentant thief who prayed to the Lord Jesus from his cross, "*Lord, remember me when Thou comest into Thy kingdom*" *(Luke 23.42)* went to be with the Lord. Jesus assured him of that, "*Today shalt thou be with Me in paradise*" *(v.43).* All who are going to be in heaven will be there, not on the basis of water (of baptism) but of blood (of

Christ). There are, however, a few difficult passages of Scripture that seem to contradict this:

**Mark 16.16: "He that believeth *and is baptized* shall be saved; but he that believeth not shall be damned"**. While the words *"and is baptized"* are included in the first half of this verse, it is noteworthy that they are not in the second half. The Lord did not say, "He that believeth not, *or is not baptized* shall be damned": this is a very significant omission! As already indicated above, there are many verses and passages in the New Testament that clearly and decisively corroborate that faith alone is essential for salvation.

**Acts 22.16: "Arise and be baptized, and wash away thy sins, calling on the name of the Lord"**. This is part of the apostle Paul's testimony to his fellow-nationals – Jews – in Jerusalem. He was quoting words spoken to him by Ananias after his conversion. The Scriptures are clear that it is the blood of Jesus Christ that cleanses from all sin *(I John 1.7)*; water can only cleanse from outward, physical defilement. Baptism is the outward and visible sign of an inward and spiritual cleansing from sin. In his Study Bible, C. C. Ryrie points out that the verse literally reads: *"having arisen, be baptized; and wash away your sins, having called on the name of the Lord"*. The washing away of Paul's sins resulted from calling on the name of the Lord, not from his baptism.

**1 Peter 3.20,21: "Baptism doth also now save us"**. When the words are taken out of their context, they certainly seem to suggest that baptism is essential to salvation! If so, they contradict the teaching of the rest of the New Testament! Since all Scripture is the word of God, there cannot be any real contradiction. We must examine the text in its context!

According to W.E. Vine, **"The like figure"** *(antitupos)* means *"corresponding type"*.[7] There are two types in **vv.20,21. Verse 20: "the ark"**, built by Noah, was the means of salvation through the flood: **"eight souls were saved by** (through) **water"**, i.e. from the judgment of God in the flood. The ark was a type or picture of Christ and the deliverance He has provided from the waves and billows of God's judgment, to which sinners are exposed. The Lord Jesus passed through the storm of judgment and, in resurrection, landed safely on the other side. Those who are *"in Christ"* - in the ark - are saved from judgment because of His death and resurrection from the dead. **Verse 21**: **"Baptism"** is another picture, corresponding to the ark. It symbolizes the death, burial and resurrection of Christ. All who are baptized express thereby that they were identified with Christ and are in Him. They are saved, not by baptism, but **"by the resurrection of Jesus Christ"**. Note the parenthesis between **"baptism doth now save us"** and **"by the resurrection of Jesus Christ".** By omitting the parenthesis, we arrive at the meaning of the verse – and of baptism: it is not baptism that saves us, but Christ, by His resurrection. The Holy Spirit, through Peter, plainly states that it is not any virtue in baptism itself that saves us: **not the putting away of the filth of the flesh"**, but what baptism symbolizes, the death and resurrection of Christ. *It is not the water of baptism in itself that effects this inward cleansing, but the saving event which baptism signifies – the resurrection of Jesus Christ in which His people share by faith" (F.F. Bruce).* [8]

1. Darby, J.N., quoted in "John Nelson Darby. A Biography by Max S. Weremchuk", (Loizeaux Brothers, Neptune, New Jersey,1992) Appendix B, p.203.
2. Willmington, H.L.: op. cit., p. 710.
3. Vine, W.E.: op. cit., "Baptize", p.50.
4. Willmington, H.L.: op. cit., p. 710.
5. Bruce, F.F.: "New London Commentary on the New Testament: The Book of the Acts", (Marshall, Morgan and Scott, Ltd., London & Edinburgh,1954), p.77.
6. Naismith, A.: "1200 Notes, Quotes and Anecdotes", (Pickering & Inglis Ltd., London, 1962) #58, p.10.
7. Vine, W.E.: op. cit.: "Figure", p.236.
8. Bruce, F.F.: "Answers to Questions", (Zondervan Publishing House, Grand Rapids, Michigan,1972) p.128.

# 4. Role of Sisters

Few subjects are more controversial today in our society (and even in some assemblies) than the role of women – whether in society in general, in the family, or in the church. The mere male who dares to address it must be unnecessarily brave to the point of being foolhardy, or even just a 'fool' – like the proverbial fool who *'rushes in where angels fear to tread '!* Or he may have firm convictions based on the word of God. It is with these convictions in mind that we approach the subject of the "Role of Sisters". Many Christians are highly critical of the supposed limitations that are placed upon women in churches where the word of God is honoured and obeyed. Among the criticisms that have been leveled at assemblies seeking to follow the Scriptural pattern and precepts are: *"Marginalized women in the assembly"; "Being a woman meant that you were to serve"* (are not we all meant to *"serve the Lord Christ"*: a most glorious privilege and high honour?); *"Insistence on head-covering".* Women are said to be *"second class citizens"* in these assemblies that remain true to the Scriptures!

At first glance, it might seem that the Bible does give women a secondary place to men. Of the 66 books in the Bible, 38 have men's names as titles; only two have women's names. Every book whose author is known was written by a male. The Old Testament story revolves largely around the masculine descendants of Adam. The tribes of Israel were all descended from the sons of Jacob, none from his daughters (Gen. 37.35; 46.7). The prophets were almost exclusively male: except Miriam *(Ex.15.20)*, Deborah *(Jud. 4.4)*, Huldah *(2 Kings 22.14)*, Noadiah *(Neh. 6.14)* and Isaiah's wife *(Is. 8.3)*. Priests were all male: Aaron, his sons and male descendants. The land of Israel was ruled by kings, except, for seven years, by the wicked queen, Athaliah. The central Character of the New Testament is the Son of God. He chose 12 as His disciples: all men. All the preachers in the Acts were men.

Yet, as we examine the Bible carefully, we discover that women in Bible times were accorded a place they did not have in the pagan society surrounding them, and still do not have in many societies today. In the Old Testament, the faith of Sarah and Rahab is recorded in Hebrews 11 along with that of Abraham and Moses; and many outstanding women are recognized and highly commended for their lives and work: e.g. Rebekah, Deborah, Ruth, Hannah, etc. In the New Testament, the Lord Jesus bestowed His gifts of healing and blessing on women equally with men; He fed women as well as men, and blessed women in His ministry: e.g. the woman at the well in Samaria *(John 4)*; the immoral woman who washed His feet with her tears *(Luke 7)*; the woman caught in adultery *(John 8)*; the woman who cast in two coins (her all) into the treasury *(Mark 12.41-44)*; Mary and Martha, etc. Women ministered to the Lord during His earthly sojourn *(Luke 8.2,3)*; and travelled with Him from Galilee to Jerusalem and all the way to Calvary *(Matt.27.55,56)*. Women were the last to leave the scene of His death and first to arrive at the empty tomb and bear the glad news of His resurrection. They are given a place of honour in the Gospel records.

In the early church, though preachers, elders, public teachers were men, yet women had a prominent place and are given honourable mention in the Acts; for example, Mary, mother of Mark *(12.12)*; Dorcas *(9.36)*; Lydia *(16.14,15)*; the honourable women of Berea *(17.12);* Priscilla (mentioned six times, with Aquila: in four of these, Priscilla is named first). In the list of 26 names in Rom.16, *Dr. Charles Ryrie* noted that Paul specifically mentioned eight women.[1] Special reference is made to *Euodias and Syntiche,* in Philippi, who worked together with Paul in the Gospel *(Phil. 4.2,3)*; to *Lois and Eunice,* the faithful grandmother and mother, respectively, of Timothy, who taught him the Scriptures *(2 Tim.1.5; 3.15)*; and to praying widows who had served diligently and faithfully *(1 Tim. 5.5,10)*.

**A. STATUS OF SISTERS IN THE CHURCH.** Christian women in the church are equal in:

**Salvation.** The blessings of salvation and eternal life, and all that accompany these glorious, God-given gifts, belong equally to men and women. *In 1 Pet. 3.7*, Peter, writing to husbands exhorts them to *"give honour unto the wife as to the weaker vessel"* – physically, *"and as being heirs together of the grace of life"* – spiritually: they share in the gift of eternal life. *Gal. 3.28* is sometimes used by evangelical feminists to prove that there is no difference between men and women in their roles and participation in the church, eliminating the divinely given authority structure indicated in 1 Cor.11.3: *"The head of the woman is the man"*. Of course, the two verses are not contradictory since both are divinely inspired. *Gal. 3.28* is not speaking at all of the relative roles of men and women in the church, but of their position by faith, through *grace:* justified *(v.24)*, children of God *(26)* and in Christ *(27)*. Differences of gender do not affect the relationship we all share in Christ.

**Church Privileges:** Men and women, equally, have the privileges of church fellowship, priesthood, prayer, mutual encouragement and service.

**Spiritual Gifts:** The Spirit of God, in His sovereign will, divides to each one, men and women, spiritual gifts to be used for the glory of God *("every man"* in *1 Cor. 12.11,* KJV, should be *"each one"*). Possibly the only gift given to men only was the gift of apostle.

**B. SERVICE OF SISTERS IN THE CHURCH.** Sisters can and do make very valuable contributions to the service of the local church: just as needful and helpful as men:

*1. Presence.* The writer to the Hebrews (**10.25**) encourages the readers, negatively, not to forsake assembling together; and, positively, to exhort, encourage one another, especially as the return of the Lord draws near. Many ladies seem to take this more to heart than do men! How many week-night meetings would be closed were it not for the sisters! How valuable and encouraging to all are their presence and inaudible prayers!

*2. Prayer.* If attendance at the weekly prayer meeting is any indication, one would have to conclude that the ladies are the prayer warriors of many assemblies. While public participation in mixed gatherings is limited to men, who can assess the value of the silent prayers of our sisters, both at the prayer-meeting and at home.

*3. Priesthood.* Again, it is the men's responsibility to exercise this privilege audibly; but all believers – including women – are priests and, as a **"holy priesthood"**, should be offering **"spiritual sacrifices" (1 Pet. 2.5)** of their praise **(Heb. 13.15)**, possessions **(Heb. 13.16; Phil.4.18)**, and persons **(Rom. 12.1)**. By their singing and silent praise, the sisters make a vital contribution to the worship at the Lord's Supper. As a "royal priesthood", they, with all the saints, have the privilege and responsibility to **"shew forth the praises** (excellencies, glories) **of Him Who hath called us out of darkness into His marvellous light" (1 Pet. 2.9)**.

*4. Spiritual Gifts.* Every believer is endowed with one or more spiritual gifts to be used in the service of the Lord in the church, for the glory of God and the blessing of men and women *(See Rom.12.6-8; 1 Cor. 12-14; Eph. 4.11,12; and 1 Pet. 4.10,11)*. Taking only the verses in **Romans.12.6-8**, we can discern several gifts that ladies can and do use with real blessing to the church:

**Ministry**, or service, does not necessarily mean public speaking. The word here is used of Phoebe, *"a servant of the church at Cenchrea" (Rom.16.1,2)*. How did she serve? By being *"a succourer* (helper) *to many"*, including Paul; and by taking the letter he wrote to the Romans: a great *"ministry"* indeed!

**Teaching**: not, for sisters, public teaching in a mixed gathering (see *1 Tim.2.12*); but teaching of younger women *(Tit. 2.3,4)* and children. Note the example of Timothy's grandmother and mother, Lois and Eunice *(2 Tim.1.5; 3.15)*.

**Exhortation**: the Greek word means *"calling to one's*

*side"* to help; and may be best translated, *"encouragement"*. How capably sisters do this!

**Giving** may include not only material possessions, but also time, and ourselves. All believers can and should give, but some have a special gift of giving. Those women who ministered to the Lord of their substance *(Luke 8.3)* were good examples of ladies who gave.

**Ruling**, unlike the others, is primarily a gift for men. The word means to stand before, to lead, and is used of elders (*1 Tim. 5.17*). In view of *1 Tim. 2.12* (to be considered later), it would only apply to ladies in their leadership of other ladies.

**Mercy** is a gift in which sisters excel! It involves, for example, visiting and caring for the sick, aged and disabled; taking meals to them; comforting the bereaved; driving patients to visit the medical doctor or hospital – or the stores. There are many ways in which this gift can be exercised to the glory of God.

5. *Talents* differ from spiritual gifts in that they are present from birth, used before conversion, possessed by unbelievers, and can be used for secular or sacred purposes. Like gifts, they should be dedicated to the Lord and used in His service for His people. Many sisters have, for example, musical ability which can be used well in the church.

6. *Care of the Home*. Young women are encouraged by Paul in Tit. 2.5 to be *"keepers at home"*; that is, workers at home, fulfilling home responsibilities; taking care of the home and those who live there; giving a welcome to those who visit. A good, well kept home is a good testimony to others outside the church.

7. *Hospitality*. **"Use hospitality one to another without grudging"** *(1 Pet. 4.9)* is an important command which women can usually obey better than men! What a blessing it is to all who visit a home, if those in the home are "given to hospitality" (Rom. 12.13)!

*8. Witnessing.* Women and men can serve the Lord effectively by their personal witness by life as well as lip; and in door-to-door visitation in the neighbourhood of the assembly building, distributing tracts and booklets and inviting residents to the services.

*9.* **Missionary Interest**. Women outnumber men on the mission-field. There are many single ladies and much fewer single men. In some countries, only women can reach women. Women at home can help missionary work by writing letters to missionaries, arranging and helping in missionary study classes and sewing classes; for example, making garments to be used on the mission-field by the nationals and in hospitals, etc.

*C. SILENCE OF SISTERS IN THE CHURCH.* Most Scriptural teaching on the silence and on the subordination of women in the church comes from the pen of the apostle Paul. As a result, he is not appreciated by many for his writings on these subjects! He has been branded a misogynist, anti-feminist, and male chauvinist, or just a "crusty old bachelor"! Many have rejected his teaching on these subjects. Others have tried to find explanations that soften or alter their real meaning. We should receive his teaching on women as we do his other writings, and, indeed, the whole Bible – as the inspired, inerrant word of God: just as inspired as *John 3.16*; just as inerrant as Paul's teaching on justification by faith; or on the Person of Christ in *Phil. 2.5-11* and *Col. 1.13-22*. If we refuse his teaching on the silence and subordination of women in the church, where do we draw the line? What about his teaching on salvation, the church, Christ, the rapture, etc. What about Peter's writings? He too wrote of women's place – in the home *(1 Pet. 3.1-6)*. Where do we stop? Should we not accept all the Scriptures as God's revelation and seek to obey them, even if we may not fully understand the reasons for their commands?

In two passages in Paul's writings, women are enjoined to be silent in church gatherings. **1 Cor. 14. 33-35** was written to a church in Corinth relatively early in his ministry and **1 Tim. 2.8-15** to an individual in Ephesus towards the end of Paul's life. Both letters were concerned with church practices.

**1 Corinthians** is a great treatise on the principles and practices of the local church. **1 Timothy** was written to give instruction on behaviour **"in the house of God, which is the church of the living God" (3.15)**. These two passages indicate a number of situations in which sisters are commanded to be silent in the church.

*1 Tim. 2.8-15.* In **verse 8**, Paul writes, **"I will that** *men* **pray everywhere..."** Two Greek words are translated *"man"* or *"men"* in the New Testament. Both are used in this chapter. One *(anthropos)* is used *"generally, 'of a human being, male or female'" (Vine* [2]). This is the word used in verses *1,4,5: 'for all* **men**... *Who will have all* **men** *to be saved... One Mediator between God and* **men.** *the* **Man** *Christ Jesus".* The other *(aner)* is used of man *"in distinction from a woman"*, *"never of the female sex"* (Vine [2]). This is the word that is used in **verse 8: "I will that** *men* **pray everywhere"**, in contrast to *"women"* (v.9); and in **verse 12: "I suffer not a** *woman* **to teach, nor to usurp authority over the** *man"*. Thus these verses prescribe two situations in the church in which women should not speak, but should be **"in silence"** (this phrase is used twice in **verses 11,12**):

*1. Prayer*: **"Men pray everywhere"**. Of course, the same apostle exhorts all, men and women, to *"pray without ceasing" (1 Thess. 5.17)*. Since 1 Timothy is written specifically to instruct regarding behaviour in the church *(3.15)*, this restriction must apply to audible participation of women in prayer in the assembly. They should, of course, be praying silently and are encouraged in **verses 9 and 10** to have their outward appearance (**"adorn themselves with modest apparel"**, etc.) and their life's activities (**"good works"**) consistent with the godliness which they profess.

2. *Teaching*: **"Let the woman learn in silence with all subjection. But I suffer not a woman to teach" (11,12)**. This seems a very clear instruction to sisters in church meetings, where men and women are present. Yet, some capable Bible students, in an endeavour to evade the obvious, have asserted that this instruction was given because the women in Ephesus, where Timothy was serving the Lord, were rather ignorant of

the Scriptures and did not understand them so were not capable of teaching! How insulting to women if that were the case! Such an interpretation contradicts the instructions given by Paul to the older women in the epistle to Titus (in Crete, where the Christians would be less mature than those at Ephesus), written at approximately the same time as 1 Timothy: *"Teach the aged (older) women...that they may teach (train) the younger women" (Tit.2.3,4).* Paul goes on to give reasons for this restriction in **1 Tim.2.13 and 14** – not because they were ignorant and could not teach; but because man was first in creation and woman was first in being deceived. *Mr. G.F. Hamilton* explained: *" Woman is not to be put into a position where she may again 'overstep' in a representative capacity, as happened in the garden." ³*

**1 Cor. 14.33-35.** "**As in all churches of the saints** (as indicated in the NIV and other translations, this phrase belongs to the verses that follow, not to verse 33), **let your women keep silence in the churches: for it is not permitted unto them to speak; but they are commanded to be under obedience, as also saith the law. And if they will learn anything, let them ask their husbands at home: for it is a shame for women to speak in the church"**. The context of these verses is the *Use of Spiritual Gifts*: a third situation in which women should be silent in the church. Note the emphasis on this: **"it is not permitted unto them to speak....it is a shame** *("disgraceful":* NIV) **for women to speak in the church"**. Could it be more explicit or emphatic? And the exhortation applies to "**all churches**", not just Corinth.

**SUBORDINATION, SUBJECTION OF SISTERS IN THE CHURCH.** The words, "subordination" and "subjection", applied to women, are repulsive to many in the 20th century, both men and women: in society in general, and in the church. They suggest discrimination and inferiority and are considered in the same category as slavery and repression. In reality, subordination does not necessarily indicate inferiority, but relates to order, whether in government, armed forces, business etc. The president of a country or business is not necessarily superior in intellect, ability, or character, etc. to the vice-president or others under him. Without order in society, there would be chaos. God has ordained certain order: for example in the home, as indicated in *Eph. 5.22-24*: *"the husband is the head of the wife... therefore as the church is subject unto Christ, so let the wives be to their own husbands in everything."* The principle of headship and corresponding subordination, in relation to the church, is clearly stated in **1 Cor. 11.3**: **"The head of every man is Christ; and the head of the woman is the man; and the head of Christ is God."** The last phrase is an important key to the subject. Christ is not inferior to God but co-equal with the Father. Voluntarily, in infinite grace, He took the place of subjection for our redemption. So, **"the head of the woman is the man"**: does not imply inferiority of woman, but her subordination to man in the church – as in the home. This order in the church is expressed in two ways:

*1. Submission* of the woman to the man. **1 Tim. 2.12**: **"I suffer not** (do not permit) **a woman to teach, nor to usurp authority over the man***"* (there is no word in the original for *"usurp"*; the Greek word means to *"exercise authority")*. This command of the Holy Spirit through Paul would exclude a sister in the church from eldership. Of course, this is also evident in the next chapter (**1 Tim. 3.2**): **"A bishop** (overseer, used interchangeably with "elder", e.g. in *Tit. 1.5,7)* **must be blameless, the *husband* of one wife"**. A woman can hardly be a *"husband"*! The Greek word translated *"husband"* denotes an adult male.

2. *Symbols*. 1 Cor.11.3-16. There are four symbols in *1 Cor.11*. The two in the second half of the chapter are easily recognizable: the bread and the cup at the Lord's Supper, representing, respectively, the body and blood of the Lord Jesus. There are also two in **verses 3-16**:

*a. The Uncovered head of the man:* vv. 4,7. A brother should not cover his head in gatherings of the Lord's people, not because it is not the custom in our culture to do so (it *was* the custom in other societies in N.T. times), but because of the command of Scripture.

i. It would be dishonouring to man's Head, Christ (**v.4**).

ii. Man **"is the image and glory of God" (v.7)** – and the glory of God should be seen, not covered.

*b. The covered head of the woman.* **vv. 5-16.** Even if there were no reasons given, sisters should be happy to obey the Lord in covering their heads. These verses state several principles that form the basic reasons for women's head-covering:

*1.* **Headship**: **vv.5,6.** Without a head-covering in a church meeting, the woman dishonours her **"head"**, that is, the man; disturbs the God-given order stated in verse 3; and ultimately dishonours Christ, Who is **"the Head of every man"**. A contradiction has been supposed between **1 Cor.11.5**, **"Every woman that prayeth or prophesieth with her head uncovered dishonoureth her head"**, and **1 Cor.14.34**, **"Let your women keep silence in the churches"**. It is obvious that a woman who prays and prophesies is not keeping silent! However, it is most unlikely that Paul would contradict himself in two verses only three chapters apart in the same letter! Moreover, this epistle is the inspired word of God, and it is impossible for God to contradict Himself! The simplest and obvious solution is that Paul, in **1 Cor.11.5,** is stating two wrongs (which do not make a right!) and immediately corrects the first: absence of head-covering, but leaves the second: praying, prophesying – i.e. speaking in the church – till **14.34**. The illustration has been used of a car speeding through red traffic-lights: the driver has committed two offences – exceeding the speed limit, and ignoring the traffic lights – which may be considered separately in his trial.

*2. Glory:* **v.7.** **"The woman is the glory of the man"**. When brothers and sisters in the Lord come together – to worship, pray, serve or learn, they should do so for the glory of God alone. The glory of the man should not be seen. Thus the woman should be covered.

*3. Creation:* **vv. 8-10.** **"For the man is not of** *(from)* **the woman; but the woman of** *(from)* **the man. Neither was the man created for the woman; but the woman for the man."**

Man was created first and woman was made from the man *(Gen. 2.21-23)* and for him. **"For this cause"**, because of the priority of man in creation, **"ought the woman to have power** (authority, and submission to it, symbolized by head-covering) **on her head."**

4. *Angels:* **v.10.** **"Because of the angels"**, who are careful observers of the church, where they learn lessons on *"the manifold wisdom of God"*, made *"known by the church" (Eph. 3.10)*. *"They are observers of God's sovereign purposes and of the way in which they are set forth in the church" (G. F. Hamilton* [4]*)*.

5. *Nature:* **vv. 13-15: "Doth not nature itself teach you..."** By the provision of long hair for women and of short hair for men (in general), nature, our God-appointed teacher instructs us that a woman's long hair is a glory for her and a covering. (Note the two "ifs": not all women have long hair, not all men have short hair; but this is the general rule). **Verse 13a, "Judge in yourselves"**: the apostle makes an appeal to the readers' own judgment and sense of propriety. **Verse 15, "her hair is given her for a covering"** does not mean she does not need a headcovering in addition; otherwise, the teaching of the whole passage would be redundant and contradictory. The word for "covering" here is different from that in **vv. 4-6.**

6. *Church and Apostolic Practice:* **v.16: "If any man seem to be contentious, we** (the apostles) **have no such custom"**: that is, there was no other apostolic practice than that which the apostle has been insisting on, namely the uncovered head of men and the covered head of women; **"neither the churches of God"**: that is, this was not only the principle for the church at Corinth but was the practice of all the churches. The N.I.V. translates: *"We have no other practice – nor do the churches of God."*

1. Ryrie, C.C.: "The Role of Women in the Church", (Moody Press, Chicago,1958), p.55.
2. Vine, W.E.: op. cit.: "Man", pp.388,389.
3. Hamilton, G.F.: "WHY?" (Christian Missions in Many Lands, Spring Lake, N.J.,1985), p.32.
4. Ibid, p.38

# 5. Government

One of the most important – but most hazardous – occupations of our time is leadership. If anything goes seriously wrong with a country, business, sports team, the person who takes the blame is the president, manager, coach. There is constant pressure on leaders to resign. Stability in government, profits in business, success in sports are all related to the quality of leadership. Leadership in the church is also very important. The Head of the church has given us, in His guide-book, the New Testament, instructions about the government of each local church: it is invested in **"elders"** whose qualifications and responsibilities – and the responsibilities of the church to them – are described in detail in the Scriptures.

The **first mention** of church elders in the New Testsment is in **Acts 11.30**, where we read that Barnabas and Saul were given a gift from the church at Antioch to take to the Christians in Judea because of a predicted famine (**v.28**). They delivered this gift to **"the elders"**. We are not told who these were nor how they were appointed.

The **first "appointment"** of elders is recorded in **Acts 14.23**. Paul and Barnabas, returning from their first missionary journey, visited each of the cities where they had planted churches, and **"ordained** (appointed for) them *elders* in every church"**. Here is the first mention of an important characteristic of New Testament churches: the plurality of *"elders"* in *"every church"*. The same feature is seen in **Acts 20.17**. Paul was now returning from his third missionary journey. Probably about a year previously, he had left Ephesus where he had spent a good part of three years *(Acts 19.8,10; 20.31)*. A good assembly was commenced, but Paul foresaw problems in the future *(Acts 20.29-32)* and had an intense desire to communicate with the *"elders* **of the** *church"* there, so sent a message for them to meet with him at the port of Miletus, about 30 miles South of Ephesus. Much later in his life, Paul, with Timothy, wrote a letter to the Philippian Christians, addressing it to *"all the saints in Christ Jesus, which are at Philippi, with the bishops and deacons"* (**1.1**). Note that the word "**bishops**" (used interchangeably with "**elders**" in the N.T.) is again plural. Similarly, Paul wrote to **Titus (1.5)**, that he had left him in Crete to *"ordain elders in every city"*.

**PLURALITY OF ELDERS**. Throughout the N.T., the same pattern is seen: a plurality of elders in each church. This is a clear and important New Testament principle, recognized by many Bible teachers today, even those who are not associated with "brethren assemblies". For example, **John Macarthur**: *"The norm in the N.T. church was a plurality of elders. There is no reference in the* N.T. *to a one-pastor congregation."*[1] **Earl Radmacher**: *"Multiple leadership was the norm in the early church."* [2] **Gene Getz**: *"Multiple leadership is a N.T. principle. The 'one man' ministry is a violation of this important guideline."*[3]

*Why Plural Leadership?* There are many good reasons:

*1.* Plurality of leaders is God's pattern set forth in His word.

*2.* Every local assembly has a variety of needs, circumstances, situations and problems, which can be met by qualified leaders who themselves have varied needs.

*3.* Elders have varied skills and abilities to deal with the different aspects of assembly work and meet the diverse needs of the Lord's people, e.g. counselling, teaching, helping, etc.

*4.* By plural leadership, the burden of the assembly is carried by several shoulders.

*5.* Leaders can sharpen one another in their spiritual lives.

*6.* Single leadership tends to pride and authoritarianism.

*7.* Single leadership can detract from the authority and sufficiency of Christ. The assembly can focus on a human leader instead of on the Lord, the Head of the church.

**PAUL'S ADDRESS TO THE ELDERS OF THE CHURCH AT EPHESUS (Acts 20.17-35)** is unique among the "sermons" recorded in the Acts. It is the only one addressed exclusively to Christians – and to a particular group of believers, elders. Note:

*THE TITLES OF ELDERS.*

*a. Elders* **(17)** – Gr., *presbuteros* (presbyter), literally means 'older' (but not necessarily 'old'; the elders in Ephesus must have been saved within the previous four years), and indicates maturity, experience, and consequent wisdom. An elder should not be "a *novice" (1 Tim. 3.6)*

*b. Overseers* **(28)**: Gr., *episkopos* (cf. 'Episcopalian'). **Acts 20.28** is one of the key N.T. verses on the subject of 'elders'. Note that these, 'overseers' were "made" by the Holy Spirit – as, indeed, are all true overseers. It is evident from this verse that **elders** – what they are – are **overseers** – what they do: look over or upon the church *(epi* = over; *scopos* = look, as in micro-, tele-scope); watch over *('supervise'*: Latin). The verb form of the word is translated *"taking the oversight"* in *1 Pet. 5.2; and "looking diligently"* in *Heb.12.15.* **Acts 20.28** is the only occasion where *episkopos* is translated *"overseer"* in the K.J.V. Three times it is translated "bishop":

*c. Bishops*: **1 Tim. 3.2, Tit.l.7, 1 Pet.2.25. In 1 Tim.3.1**, *"the office of a bishop"* (KJV) is really *"overseership"*. In **Tit.1.7**, the word, **'bishop'** (KJV) is used interchangeably with **"elders" (v.5)**, again showing that **elders** are *bishops* or **overseers.** In Christendom, a bishop is usually over several 'churches'. In the New Testament, there are several 'bishops' in each church. In **1 Pet. 2.25**, the Lord Jesus is described as **"the Shepherd and Bishop of our souls."** He is our true and only Archbishop!

*d. Shepherds:* (28). This word does not occur here in the KJV, but other translations, e.g. the NIV, have **"be shepherds"** instead of **"feed"**. Five other Greek words are translated **'feed'** in the KJV New Testament: meaning: to give food to, nourish. The Greek word here *is poimaino,* which is the verb form of the word "shepherd" and involves more than feeding; it includes all that a shepherd does for his flock of sheep. Indeed, in the same verse and in *v.29*, Paul used the word *"flock"*, another form of the same word, in keeping with the shepherd character of the overseer. It should be noted that the word *"over* the which" (KJV): is the Greek 'en' = 'in', translated **"among"** in **1 Pet. 5.2**: **"Feed** (shepherd) **the flock of God which is** among **you"**. Peter, in 1 Pet. 5.1,2, used the same terminology as in **Acts 20.17,28: "elders...feed** (shepherd)**...taking the oversight** (overseers)."

*e. Pastors*: The word only occurs once in the KJV New Testament, in *Eph. 4.11*, but it is the same word as is translated "shepherds" elsewhere, for example in the story of the *shepherds* who kept watch over their flocks by night in the vicinity of Bethlehem when Jesus was born *(Luke 2.8)*. Since elders are shepherds of the flock, we could well call every elder a "pastor". Since there should be a plurality of elders in each local church, there should obviously be a plurality of pastors.

**THE TRIALS OF ELDERS.** The task of an elder is no sinecure! It involves much more than attending 'oversight meetings' once a month! Those who take responsibility for oversight in the local church should recognize the problems involved. Just as a shepherd has to be prepared for disease, dangers and death affecting the sheep, so the godly pastor has to be alert for trials. These may come from two different sources:

*a. From Without, External* **(29): "I know this, that after my departure shall grievous wolves enter in among you, not sparing the flock".** Paul continued to use the analogy of elders as shepherds, feeding God's flock. In many countries, the great danger for sheep is the entry of savage wolves among them (see *John 10.12*). Likewise, Paul foresaw the invasion of fierce 'wolves' into the church at Ephesus. We know a little of the subsequent history of the church at Ephesus from the epistles to Timothy who had been left at Ephesus *(1 Tim.1.3)* to deal with problems that would arise there, and from the Lord's own letter to the church at Ephesus *(Rev. 2.1-7),* which shows that they had *"left"* – abandonned their *"first love"*. The ferocious wolves of Paul's time might include Judaizing teachers coming in from without, false philosophies, gnosticism, etc. There are all kinds of 'wolves' today that try to invade God's flock and work havoc among His people: secular humanism, New Age philosophies, financial allurements, and even such things as TV and other entertainment. The 19th century preacher, Henry Ward Beecher; told of a mother in wild frontier country, who was, one day, washing clothes by a stream, while her only child was playing nearby. Suddenly she realized he was no longer near her. She called his name but there was no answer. She ran to her home: he was not there. In wild distress, she dashed to the forest. There she found the child but it was too late! The child had been killed by a wolf! Heartbroken, she picked up the child's lifeless body and tenderly carried it home. Beecher concluded: *"Oh how that mother hated wolves!"* So should we: especially elders!

*b. From Within: Internal* **(30): "Also of your own selves shall men arise, speaking perverse things, to draw away disciples after them."** Paul was predicting that from within the church, perhaps even from the group of elders then visiting him, there would arise false teachers who would distort, corrupt and twist the truth with the purpose of drawing away followers. This evidently happened in Ephesus in Paul's lifetime. The two epistles to Timothy were written to combat those errors, to warn of false teachers who were already teaching heretical doctrines, and had turned against Paul *(2 Tim.1.15).* In these epistles, Paul exhorted Timothy to *"give attendance"*, *"take heed"* to *"doctrine"*, and to emphasize *"sound doctrine"*, *"good doctrine" (1 Tim. 1.3,10; 4.13,16; 6.3; 2 Tim. 4.2,3).* These exhortations are equally valid for us today as we see, in churches everywhere, and even in assemblies, departure from the word of God in relation to its inspiration and inerrancy, the Person of Christ, and the principles of the N.T. church. Elders and all of us should beware!

*THE TASKS OF ELDERS.* Faced with such problems,

111

what are the responsibilities of shepherds of the flock of God? From Paul's exhortations to the elders in this address, and his own example while he was with them, we can discern four tasks of elders:

*a. Watch* **(31)**. **"Therefore watch"**, literally, *'keep awake'*, be alert spiritually, *"be vigilant" (1 Pet.5.8:* same word). This watchful attitude of elders is suggested by the title *"overseers"*. Each elder should watch in four directions:

*1.* **"Yourselves" (28): "Take heed unto yourselves".** **"Take heed"** is not the same word as **"watch"**, but it has similar implications: turn attention to, regard, 'take care': sometimes said casually as a farewell greeting, but here intended very seriously! Elders – and all of us - should carefully watch our own lives: **"Yourselves"** first; not that they are more important! Not to encourage self centredness! But we can never be a blessing to others if we are careless about our own testimony. If elders neglect their personal spirituality, their service on behalf of others will not count for very much!

*2.* **"All the flock" (28): "And to all the flock, over** (in) **the which the Holy Ghost hath made you overseers".** The writer to the Hebrews, in the last chapter of his epistle, draws the attention of readers to their responsibilities to their leaders or guides *("them that have the rule over* you": KJV: *13.7,17,24),* but also indicates the responsibilities of the leaders, one of which is: *"they watch for your souls as they that must give account' (13.17).* Their concern for the spiritual wellbeing of the flock should be such that they **"watch"**: literally 'chase sleep', are sleepless: like a nurse in the intensive care unit, monitoring the vital signs of an ill patient; or a wakeful shepherd watching the flock and guarding from vicious wolves.

The mention of the "flock" reminds us again that each elder is a shepherd, responsible to watch the sheep, and to give to the church of God the same care that a good shepherd gives to his sheep. This responsibility is beautifully illustrated in the care *"the good Shepherd"* gives to all His sheep, as seen *in Psalm 23* and *John 10.1-18,28.* It can also be illustrated, by default, in the failure of Israel's shepherds – kings, prophets, priests – to tend the sheep in their care: see **Ezekiel 34.1-10.** The responsibility to the flock includes: **Nutrition:** *"Ye feed not the flock" (vv.2,3,8b);* **Recuperation** from sickness: *"the diseased have ye not strengthened, neither have ye healed that which was sick" (4);* **Consolation:** *"neither have ye bound up that which was broken" (4),* including broken hopes, hearts, homes, families, marriages, etc.; **Restoration:** *"neither have ye brought again that which was driven away" (4);* **Investigation:** *"neither have ye sought that which was lost"* (4); **Protection:** *"Because there is no shepherd... they became meat to all the beasts of the field when they were scattered" (5,8);* to which should be added, **Intercession.** These false shepherds certainly neglected it; but our Chief Shepherd is also our great High Priest Who *"maketh intercession for us" (Rom. 8.34).*

3. **"Grievous wolves...therefore watch" (29,31).** They come in various forms and disguises, and elders have to be constantly on the alert, lest they come upon the flock unawares.

4. **"Of your own selves shall men arise...therefore watch" (30,31).** Perhaps the most difficult and dangerous problems arise from within the church. Elders: beware!

*b. Warn* **(31): "Remember, that by the space of three years I ceased not to warn every one night and day".** What an example Paul had left these elders! What a contrast to the cruel and callous 'shepherds' of Israel, described in *Ezek.34!* His example was seen, not only in the life he had lived before them **(vv.18-21)** but in the way he, as an overseer, had discharged his responsibilities and warned them of coming dangers. All elders should follow his example and warn the flock – God's people – of the enemy of souls, who *"as a roaring lion, walketh about seeking whom he may devour" (1 Pet. 5.8)* and of the *"wolves"* he uses.

*c. Weep* **(31): "With tears".** Paul had a shepherd's heart, with a genuine care for the sheep under his care. He followed the Good Shepherd, Who wept while on earth *(John 11.35)*. He could well say, *"Be ye followers of me even as I also am of Christ" (1 Cor.11.1)*. Do we have that kind of compassion – when a child of God has fallen into sin, or is passing through a serious crisis in life, or is being led astray by false teachers?

    *d. Work* **(34,35): "These hands have ministered unto my necessities, and to them that were with me. I have showed you...how that so laboring ye ought to support the weak and remember the words of the Lord Jesus, how He said, 'It is more blessed to give than to receive'"**. Paul's working for his own support and that of his colleagues was an example to the elders, that their task should be done without thought of material reward.

    *THE TRUST OF ELDERS* **(32).** How can elders carry out the great responsibility of shepherding the flock of God? *"Who is sufficient for these things?" (2 Cor. 2.16) "Our sufficiency is of God" (2 Cor. 3.5)*. It is to Him Paul directed these elders – and us today. Whether we are elders or not, our **trust** must be, not in ourselves, but in:

1. **God**: not in men, however godly or gifted. Paul was both but he did not commend these elders to himself but to God: **"I commend you to God"** Who is faithful and unchangeable. *"My God shall supply all your need according to His riches in glory by Christ Jesus" (Phil.4.19)*.

2. **The Word**: which is infallible, inerrant, immutable. Here are all the resources needed for all the problems and trials confronting elders at all times. False teaching should be tested by the touchstone of "the *Holy Scriptures which are able to make...wise" (2 Tim.3.15)*.

3. **His Grace**: which, as Paul had learned, *"is sufficient"* for any trial or weakness *(2 Cor.12.9)* and for every crisis in every church and in every Christian.

*RECOGNITION OF ELDERS*. How are elders recognized? Note three important principles of Scripture:

    *a.* Elders are made **by the Holy Spirit** *(Acts 20:28)*: they are not man-made or self made. Only those made – appointed – by the Holy Spirit are truly elders.

*b.* Elders are primarily responsible to the Lord, *"the Shepherd and Bishop* (Overseer) *of...souls" (1 Pet.2.25),* to Whom *"they must give account"* (Heb.13.17). They are, secondarily, accountable to the local church where they serve, and to their fellow-elders.

*c.* Elders should be **acknowledged by the local church:** *"Know (recognize, appreciate) them which labour among you and are over you in the Lord and admonish you" (1 Thess. 5.12).*

Elders may be recognized by:

*1.* **Desire for the work,** not the position. **"If a man desire the office of a bishop, he desireth a good work (1 Tim. 3.1).** As already noted, "the office of a bishop" is the translation of one Greek word meaning 'overseership': it is not really desire for the office but for the **good work** of oversight. Since the work is caring for the saints, this desire is really the result of deep concern for the welfare of God's people.

*2.* **Doing the work.** A person who is to be recognized as an elder will already have been observed to be doing the work an elder should do.

*3.* **Spiritual Qualifications:** not intellectual brilliance, social position, financial fitness or pleasing personality; but spiritual qualities as outlined in **1 Tim. 3.1-7** and **Tit. 1.6-9.** As each elder is *"the steward of God"* (Tit. 1.7) entrusted, not only with God's work but with God's people, he is required to be very special in his character and behaviour. Of course, since all believers are stewards, these characteristics should be seen in all of us! They can be subdivided as follows:

*a.* **Personal.** Some characteristics are general, for example, *Blameless:* above reproach; *Holy; Just; Of good behaviour:* orderly. Others are specific and closely related to:

115

**Wine.** Negatively, *Not given to wine.* Positively, *Sober, Vigilant.* In the Old Testament, Aaron and his sons, priests, were commanded, *"Do not drink wine nor strong drink.. when ye go into the tabernacle of the congregation, lest ye die: it shall be a statute for ever."* It is noteworthy that this command followed immediately after the death of Nadab and Abihu, Aaron's first two sons, who had *"offered strange fire before the Lord"* and died. It seems likely that they were drunk *(Lev.10.1-3,9)*. Some of the other negative personal characteristics of elders may be the consequences of wine, for example, *"No striker...not a brawler"*.

**Money.** *"Not greedy of filthy lucre"*: base gain (financial or otherwise); *"Not covetous"*.

**Temper.** *"No striker"; "Not a brawler"; "Not soon angry"; "Temperate"*.

*b.* **Domestic.** *"Husband* of (but) *one* wife": literally *'a one-woman man'*. This confirms that an elder must be masculine, but does not mean that he must be married, nor that he may not remain an elder if he should remarry after the death of his spouse. He should, however, have only one wife at a time, and should not have close relationships with other women. *"Ruleth well his own house"* – otherwise, *"how shall he take care of the church of God?" "Having his children in subjection with all gravity"* – giving him proper respect. *"Having faithful children not accused of riot or unruly." "Given to hospitality"*, a characteristic of all Christians: see *Rom.12.13; 1 Pet. 4.9; Heb.13.2.*

*c.* **Ecclesiastical**: in relation to the church. *"Apt* (able) *to teach"*, not necessarily from a pulpit. It implies a knowledge of the Word and ability to instruct others, whether in a small or large group, or individually. All elders, whether with the specific gift of teaching or not, should be men of the Book, reading it and studying it for their own spiritual lives and for the instruction of the "flock" whom they are to "feed" (shepherd). *"Take care of the church of God"*: this involves forethought and provision; like the "Good Samaritan" who treated his patient, brought him to an inn and *"took care of him"*

*(Luke 10.34,35*: the only other occasions where the word, *"take care"* is used in the N.T.). *"Lover of good* (men)".

*d.* **Social:** in relation to the world. *"Blameless":* applies to every sphere of an elder's life. Charges laid against an elder mar the testimony of the whole assembly. *"Must have a good report of them that are without"* – in the neighbourhood, business, employment, etc. *"lest he fall into reproach and the snare of the devil":* how quickly Satan seizes on any delinquency of God's people, especially elders and those who preach and teach! W E. Vine comments, *"If a man has brought reproach upon the testimony by a single act, his restoration to the fellowship of the church is possible and should be sought for, but his readmission as an overseer is quite another thing and should not be attempted."* [4] In rare instances, when there has been evident, genuine repentance, full restoration may be possible after some time.

*e.* **Scriptural:** in relation to the Word: *"Apt to teach"; "Holding fast the faithful word" (Tit.1.9):* cleaving to its doctrines, principles and practices; so *"able by* (in) *sound doctrine to exhort"* **believers;** and *"to convince* (refute) *the gainsayers"* – those who oppose, **unbelievers.**

**RESPONSIBILITIES OF THE CHURCH TO THE ELDERS.** The sheep in the "flock of God" have responsibilities, not only to the "Chief Shepherd" but also to the under-shepherds who "feed the flock". These may be summarized as follows:

1. *Know* them **(1 Thess. 5.12)**. Recognize, appreciate, value them.
2. *Consider* them **(Heb.13.7).** Contemplate and carefully observe their way of life.
3. *Follow* them **(Heb.13.7)**. Imitate their faith and faithfulness.
4. *Obey, Submit* to them **(Heb.13.17; 1 Pet.5.5)**, recognizing their God-given authority. If their instructions conflict with the word of God, *"we ought to obey God rather than men". (Acts 5.29)*

5. *Respect and Honour* them: **"Salute them" (Heb.13.24).** Greet, acknowledge with respect.

6. *Remember* them **(Heb.13.7)**. Recall the way they lived, the words they spoke.

7. *Pray* for them. Every diligent, faithful elder has heavy responsibilities, time-consuming tasks, and a great burden of care! They all need divine strength and grace and the prayer support of all the saints. If we pray more and complain less, we shall be better served!

1. MacArthur, John F., Jr.: "Answering the Key Questions About Elders" (Word of Grace Communications, Panorama City, 1984), p.27.
2. Radmacher, Earl D.: "The Question of Elders" (Western Baptist Press, Portland, 1977), p.5.
3. Getz, Gene: "Sharpening the Focus of the Church" (Moody Press, Chicago, 1974), p.121.
4. Vine, W.E.: "The Epistles to Timothy and Titus" (Oliphants, London, 1965), p.55.

# 6. Church Discipline

**"Church Discipline"** is a touchy and difficult subject – to speak about, write about, and, especially, to carry out! Frequently, family and friends of the person disciplined are very offended and may resign from church fellowship, leading, in some cases, to division in the assembly. Even more seriously, a case of church discipline can result in disturbing lawsuits, widespread reporting of the problem and awards of large sums of money to the disciplined party. In 1987, two eminent U.S. Christian lawyers, Lynn Buzzard and Thomas S. Brandon, Jr., wrote a book, *"Church Discipline and the Courts"*, based mainly on a suit against a small church in Oklahoma, U.S.A., which resulted in a $390,000 judgment; and quoting other cases involving suits of one, three and even ten million dollars! On the front cover of the book, the question is asked, *"Does a church have the legal right to reprimand and expel members whose behaviour is willfully unbiblical?"* On the back cover: *"It's in the headlines all over the country. People faced with church discipline are suing the church – and winning – like never before. What are the church's legal rights? Can the church continue to practice discipline as described in Scripture? Which cases are winning in court and why? How can the church protect itself against lawsuits? How likely is this to happen at your church? Church discipline has been practiced throughout history, and until recently the right has not been questioned. Now suddenly this matter has jumped to the forefront and become a controversial problem as churches struggle to balance their theology with the reality of lawsuits."*[1]

To discipline those guilty of serious sin is clearly a command of Scripture, which the church is required to obey. How can this be done without incurring prohibitive costs in lawsuits? What precautions should be taken?

*WHAT IS DISCIPLINE?* What do you understand by church discipline? What is the nature of discipline, and when should it be exercised? To many, the word 'discipline' suggests excommunication from the church, resulting from serious sexual immorality. Biblical church discipline is, however, much wider than that, and there are several different ways of exercising it, including exclusion from fellowship.

**"Discipline"**, according to dictionary definition, conveys the idea of training with a view to developing proper conduct, and includes *"punishment inflicted by way of correction and training."* A secondary meaning is *"a branch of instruction or learning":* for example, history, science, medicine.[2]

In the K.J.V. Bible, the word *"discipline"* occurs only once – in *Job 36.10: "He openeth also their ear to **discipline**. and commandeth that they return from iniquity."* In the NIV, the word *'discipline'* here is translated *'correction'.* The original Hebrew word translated 'discipline' is elsewhere translated, in the KJV, *'correction', 'instruction', 'chastening', 'chastisement',* etc. In the NIV, *'discipline'* occurs 39 times in the Old Testament, and 13 times in the New: including ten times in Heb.12.5-11, replacing the KJV: *"chasten-ing,* -eth, -ed" (5,6 7,10,11), *'chastisement'* (8), *'corrected'* (9).

*HEB.12.5-11:* The subject in these verses is not church discipline, but family discipline, God's training of His own children: note the words, **"My son"**, **"every son"**, **"what son"**. But there are principles in these verses that apply to discipline in the church of God. For example, the Lord disciplines us because He loves us: **"Whom the Lord loveth He chasteneth" (6).** Likewise, in the church – as in the home – discipline should be always in love. Training of a child does not necessarily involve 'spanking', but sometimes spanking is needed! So, in God's family, punishment is sometimes needed – He *"scourgeth* (NIV, *punishes)* **every son whom He receiveth" (6).** 'Scourging' may also be involved in church discipline. God's discipline is always purposeful. Our earthly fathers **"for a few days chastened us after their own pleasure; but He for our profit, that we might be partakers of His holiness"**

**(10).** This, too, is one of the objectives of discipline in the local church: that we might be holy like our heavenly Father. The church is a training centre, where the Word is taught and the principles of holy, godly living are explained. If these lessons are carefully taught, not only from the platform but by elders and others in the assembly in their lives and contacts with the believers, fewer problems will arise requiring corrective discipline. Though child discipline may not be pleasant – but **"grievous"** at the time – ultimately it is beneficial, if administered in the right way. So, discipline in the church, while temporarily painful and hurting, is designed to **"yield the peaceable fruit of righteousness" (11).**

What a serious responsibility it is to administer discipline in a local church! How important that such a delicate task be undertaken faithfully and compassionately by godly, spiritual elders, in a spirit of humility and with Christlike love! Discipline should always be with a view to restoration. The objective is to heal, not to hurt, although sometimes hurting is necessary for healing. Sinning saints, like wandering sheep and foolish children must sometimes smart under *"the rod of discipline" (Prov.22.15, NIV)*

***WHY? REASONS and PURPOSES FOR CHURCH DISCIPLINE.*** Basically and primarily, church discipline is carried out because the Lord has commanded it in His word. Unfortunately and sadly – in many local churches, discipline is seriously neglected. Our godly love and concern for His people must not cause us to compromise God's truth, disobey His explicit commands nor lower biblical standards. Every assembly that recognizes the authority of the word of God has a responsibility to follow its instructions, however difficult or unpleasant this may be on some occasions. **Sin and error must be dealt with:**

*1.* **To maintain and uphold the purity and holiness of the church** and thus preserve its testimony for the Lord. **"That we might be partakers of His holiness" (Heb.12.10).** *"Holiness becometh Thine house, O Lord, for ever" (Ps. 93.5).* Since every local church is *"the house of God" (1 Tim. 3.15),* indwelt by the Holy Spirit *(1 Cor. 3.16)* holiness should be maintained and displayed in each church. *"Be ye holy for I am holy"(1 Pet.1.16)*. The awesome holiness of God was impressed upon Israel early in their journey from Egypt, by the deaths of *Nadab and Abihu* when they *"offered strange fire before the Lord' (Lev. 10.1,2);* and upon the church early in her history, by the deaths of *Ananias and Sapphira (Acts 5.1-11)*.

*2.* **To prevent the spread of evil among God's people.** A key N.T. chapter on church discipline is **1 Cor. 5,** where Paul gave this important reason: **"Know ye not that a little leaven leaveneth the whole lump? Purge out therefore the old leaven (6,7).** *"Leaven"* in Scripture speaks of malice (evil) and wickedness **(8)** in life or teaching *(Matt.16.11,12).* **"Therefore let us keep the feast** *(festival:* not the Lord's Supper, nor the Passover, but the continuous life of the believer – and the church), **not...with the leaven of malice and wickedness but with the unleavened bread of sincerity and truth"** (1 Cor. 5.8).

*3.* **As a warning and deterrent to others.** 1 Tim. 5.20: **"Them that sin rebuke before all, that others also may fear".** What Paul wrote in the context of elders, and with them specifically in view, is clearly applicable to all in the church who are guilty of serious sin.

*4.* **To bring about the repentance of the sinning believer, and restoration to the Lord and to the fellowship of the local church.** In **1 Cor. 5,** the apostle urged the discipline of a brother who had sinned very seriously **(1-5,13).** When he wrote 2 Corinthians, probably later in the same year (55 A.D.), it seems that the erring brother had shown genuine sorrow and repentance, so Paul urged forgiveness and restoration to fellowship **(2 Cor. 2.5-11).**

*5.* **To vindicate the name of the Lord and bring honour and glory to Him.** Every believer should echo the sentiments of David who said: *"Lord, I have loved the habitation of Thy house, and the place where Thine honour dwelleth" (Ps. 26.8).* Since *"the habitation of Thy house"* is a description of each local church *(1 Cor. 3.16)*, we should love the church and be concerned when dishonour is brought upon God's name by the toleration of sin and evil in an assembly of God's people.

**WHEN? WHAT? OCCASIONS AND METHODS OF CHURCH DISCIPLINE.** Exclusion from church fellowship is by no means the only form of Scriptural church discipline. The following are some New Testament examples of occasions and modes of church discipline:

*Personal Offence: Reconciliation.* **Matt.18.15-17.** Verse **17** contains the second and third references to **"the church"** in the Bible, the first being in *Matt.16.18,* where the Lord spoke of the church in its universal aspect. In *Matt.18*, it is clear that He referred to the local church. His words, **"If thy brother shall trespass *against thee"* (15)**, would seem to indicate that He is speaking about a personal offence between two Christians (although some manuscripts and translations do not have *'against thee'*). The principles enunciated by the Lord in dealing with such an offence may be applied in other circumstances where discipline is required. The Lord gave four steps to be followed by the offended person to effect reconciliation between the two parties:

*1.* Go to the offender personally, and, prayerfully and graciously, **"tell him his fault between thee and him alone" (15).** If he acknowledges it, repents and seeks forgiveness, then **"thou hast gained thy brother"**: no further action is needed: Case closed! Note that, at this stage, it is **"between thee and him alone"**: not telling others, even elders!

2. **"If he will not hear thee, take with thee one or two more..." (16)** reliable witnesses. Again, if the sinning person repents, the case is closed. If not:

3. **"Tell it unto the church" (17)**, presumably to a responsible brother, an elder of the church, to deal with the problem. If the offender humbly acknowledges his wrong, no more need be done. If not, however, there is one final step, church discipline:

*4.* **"Let him be unto thee as an heathen man and a publican" (17),** that is, outside the local church. The Lord seems to be saying that the unrepentant brother is to be excommunicated from the church. Since, however, heathen and publicans are to be won for Christ, the brother, when repentant, should be restored to church fellowship. An alternative interpretation, in view of the words "unto thee": **"Let him be *unto thee* as a heathen man..."**, is that he is excluded, not from church fellowship, but from personal fellowship – with the brother against whom he sinned.

**Temporary Lapse: Restoration. Gal. 6.1.** When a believer is **"overtaken in a fault"**, that is, found "off guard", tripped up, "caught in a sin" (NIV) – not a deliberate, premeditated sin, nor persistence in a course of sin – such a person is to be **"restored"** by a **"spiritual"** Christian in a spirit of meekness. The word **"restored"** was used of setting a fractured bone or dislocated joint. Similarly, gentle and patient handling is necessary to restore such a person to normal activity and service.

*Disorderly Conduct, Insubordination, Idleness: Warning, Withdrawal.* **1 Thess. 5.14; 2 Thess. 3.6-15.** Paul seems to have been referring to the same individuals in both passages. The adjective translated **"unruly"** in **1 Thess. 5.14** corresponds to the adverb **"disorderly"** in **2 Thess. 3.6 and 11**, and to the verb translated **"behaved not ourselves disorderly"** in **2 Thess. 3.7**. It is a military term, meaning *"out of rank or order".* In the context, Paul was referring to some who were idle, possibly because of their expectation of Christ's second coming, and refused to work **(2 Thess. 3.8-11)**. Instead of being busy, they were **"busybodies"**. Such persons, and others who refuse to heed instruction, should be "warned" **(1 Thess. 5.14)**, that is, admonished (as in v.12 = warned and instucted). If they do not respond, the believers should **"withdraw"** themselves from them **(2 Thess. 3.6)** – avoid them; give them 'the cold shoulder'.

*Trouble-making, Vain (idle) Talking: Silence. Rebuke.* Tit.1.10-14. Those who persist in causing trouble and deceiving others by teaching error should be sharply rebuked and silenced.

*Divisiveness: Warning, Rejection, Avoidance.* **Rom. 16.17; Tit. 3.10.** From the early days of the church, it is evident that there were those who caused divisions and factions, resulting in disunity and marring of the testimony. They are still with us! The word translated **"heretic"** in Tit. 3.10 refers to such persons. They should be given two **"admonitions"** and, if unresponsive, should be **"rejected"**, probably from church fellowship; certainly from any public place in the church. In **Rom. 16.17**, Paul commands the readers to **"avoid them"**.

*Public Sin: Public Rebuke.* **1 Tim. 5.20. "Them that sin rebuke before all, that others also may fear."** While this is in the context of elders in the church, the principle is applicable to all believers in the church who sin publicly, but whose sin is not sufficiently serious to warrant excommunication. The tense of the verb **"sin"** indicates persistent sinning (Vine[3]). The rebuke will be a deterrent to others, who will **"fear"**.

*Serious Moral Sins: Excommunication.* **1 Cor. 5.** This chapter begins by describing a case of very serious moral sin (a man who was living in an adulterous relationship with his stepmother), which had evidently not been judged. Indeed, the Corinthians, instead of grieving over the sin, were **"puffed up"** - proud that they could tolerate such sin in the assembly! Paul pointed out the seriousness of having such a person continuing in fellowship (**vv. 3-8**) and urged the Corinthians to **"purge out the old leaven"** by excluding the **"wicked person"** from church fellowship (**13**), and also from social fellowship with the believers (**11**). **Verses 10 and 11** give a list of serious sins which similarly require excommunication:

**Sexual Immorality: "Fornication"** includes all sexual immorality.

**Covetousness:** greed, evidenced in such ways as stealing, gambling.

**Extortion:** rapacious, inordinately greedy: open dishonesty, misappropriation of funds.

**Idolatry**: turning back from God to idol-worship.

**Railing**: public abuse, slander, defamation of character, violent language.

**Drunkenness**: habitual.

Each case should be considered individually. If the sin is publicly known, it should be dealt with publicly. When there is evidence of repentance and restoration to the Lord, the sinning believer should be forgiven and restored to church fellowship (**2 Cor. 2.5-11**).

*Serious Doctrinal Errors: Excommunication.* **2 John 9-11; 1 Tim. 1.19,20; 2 Tim. 2.17,18.** Those who teach heresy, denying the fundamental doctrines of the Christian faith – especially in regard to the Person of Christ – are also to be rejected from church fellowship unless and until they give evidence of repentance and retract the false teaching. John (**2 John 10**) commanded that visitors who did not "bring this doctrine" should not be received into the home, let alone the church. **"This doctrine"** was **"the doctrine of Christ"**, which may mean the teachings of Christ recorded in the Gospels, or the teaching regarding the Person of Christ. The latter seems more likely in view of **verse 7, "Many deceivers are entered into the world who confess not that Jesus Christ is come in the flesh"**. Paul wrote about Hymenaeus in **1 Tim. 1.20 and 2 Tim. 2.17** (probably the same person), who denied the truth of the resurrection, a fundamental doctrine of the faith. He had **"delivered him to Satan"**, the expression used in *1 Cor. 5.5* of the excommunication of the Corinthian offender.

*HOW? MANNER OF CHURCH DISCIPLINE.* In giving his command to the Corinthians to **"put away"** the **"wicked person"** who had been guilty of serious immorality, Paul introduced his statement by the phrase, **"when ye are gathered together"** (**1 Cor. 5.4**). Discipline, then, is to be carried out by the whole church, not just by the elders – though they have the responsibility to decide when and how it should be done and to make the public announcement to the assembled church.

# CHURCH DISCIPLINE

This is always a very serious matter, not to be taken lightly or spoken about flippantly. The following principles should be adhered to in all cases of discipline:

*1.* Discipline should always be based on confirmed facts – not just rumour, suspicion or hearsay. It is advisable to seek the confession of the sinning person – in the presence of witnesses; or, failing this, the testimony of one or more reliable witnesses.

*2.* Discipline should always be carried out with humility and meekness *(Gal.6.1)*, and with love and sorrow *(1 Cor.5.2: "And have not rather mourned"; NIV: "Shouldn't you rather have been filled with grief?").*

*3.* Strict confidentiality should be observed at all times, making sure that information given in confidence is not disclosed.

If an individual in assembly fellowship hears something about another believer in the same fellowship that may require disciplinary action, he/she should go to the individual concerned and deal with it privately if possible. Failing this, he/she should consult an elder about the matter, still maintaining confidentiality.

***CHURCH DISCIPLINE AND THE LAW COURTS.*** In view of the increasing incidence of filing of lawsuits by church members who have been disciplined, and the phenomenal rise in the amounts of awards sought and obtained in the courts, it is obvious that great care is required in handling all cases of discipline in the local church. Church discipline is commanded in Scripture so is mandatory for every assembly that recognizes the Bible as the authoritative word of God. Since it has been found that in most (if not all) cases that go to trial by judge and jury, the jury files against the church, it is advisable to do whatever is necessary to stay out of the courts.

"Prevention is better than cure" applies to more than medical matters! The following guidelines for protecting assemblies against lawsuits and handling disciplinary problems, even before they arise, have been obtained from two main sources:

*"Church Discipline and the Courts"*, by *Lynn R. Buzzard* and *Thomas S. Brandon,* Jr. (Tyndale House Publishers, Inc., Wheaton, Illinois. January,1987).

*"Court Involvement in Church Discipline"*, by *Jay A. Quine,* Lawyer and Pastor (Two Articles in "Bibliotheca Sacra", January-March and April-June,1992).

*1.* Each local church should be incorporated. This is a 'protective shield', which does not infringe on the beliefs and practices of the church. Although many assemblies are handled by trusteeship, the opinion of experts in law is that formal incorporation is more beneficial in cases of lawsuits.

*2.* Every assembly should have an up-to-date membership list. Obviously, only "church members" (that is, those who are officially "in fellowship") should be subject to discipline.

*3.* Every assembly should have a written discipline policy which should be included in the assembly's *"Statement of Faith and Practice"*, taught publicly in the church, and consistently followed in the practice of the church, without partiality or respect of persons.

*4.* Each church "member" – including everyone subsequently received into fellowship – should be required to sign that they have read, understood and agreed with the statement of disciplinary practice. This signed copy should be kept on file. Thus no one will be able to plead ignorance of the church's principles and practices. At intervals, the attention of the church should be drawn to the church's policy on discipline.

*5.* When a case arises, which may require discipline, representative elders should interview the "guilty party" and others who may be involved, to ascertain the veracity of the facts presented. Such interviews should be in love and non-confrontational. Gossip should be corrected and rumour-mongers may have to be rebuked, publicly if necessary. Written records of all interviews and counselling sessions should be kept.

*6.* When discipline is required, an announcement should be made only to "members" of the assembly: either at a special meeting of the assembly called for this purpose, or after the Lord's Supper (or other gathering for those in fellowship only), visitors and children having been asked to leave before the announcement is made.

7. The announcement should be made with discretion, making it clear that this is of concern to all members – and only to members. The statement should be carefully prepared and read. It is wise to have a "standard" statement composed before the need arises, which can be used as a guide, the wording being altered as necessary in individual cases. Care should be taken to ensure that the announcement to the assembly is factual and truthful, confirmed by the admission of the disciplined person and/or the testimony of reliable witnesses.

8. The person (presumably, an elder) making the announcement should warn the congregation that the information is confidential and should not be talked about among other believers, and certainly not mentioned outside the assembly.

CONCLUSION: Exercising church discipline is never easy, and always sad, and can lead to difficulties in the assembly and, occasionally, with the law. If, however, it is done carefully, wisely, in love and in accordance with the principles of God's word, and observing the above guidelines, it will bring glory to the Lord and lead to blessing in the church and restoration of the one disciplined.

1. Buzzard, Lynn R.& Brandon, Thomas S. Jr.: "Church Discipline and the Courts" (Tyndale House Publishers, Inc., Wheaton Illinois,1986).
2. "The Random House Dictionary of the English Language. The Unabridged Edition" (Random House, New York,1966).
3. Vine, W.E.: "The Epistles to Timothy and Titus" (Oliphants, London,1965), p.86.

# 7. Where are we going?

These studies have concerned the heritage that has been passed on, through many generations, to us living in the closing years of the 20th century A.D. Primarily, they have come to us right from the word of God and the days of the New Testament. In particular, we have been concerned with the truths and principles of the church in the New Testament that were rediscovered in the mid-1820's, in the days of Edward Cronin, John G. Bellett, Lord Congleton, John Nelson Darby, Anthony Norris Groves and others. The movement that started with these men in Britain also commenced, almost simultaneously, in other parts of the world. It is still going on throughout the globe. At the beginning of our studies, we asked the question, **"Where did we come from?"** In this final study, our subject is, **"Preserving the Heritage"**, and our question, **"Where are we going?"**

**"Where are we going?"** Perhaps the first and simplest answer that springs to mind is, "We're going home! To glory! To be with Christ for ever!" In my early days in Sunday School in Scotland, we used to sing a chorus, *"I'm going home in the morning train, evermore with Christ to reign, for my sins are all taken away, taken away!"* At this point, let's pause and ask the reader, "Are you on that road that leads home to heaven? Are you sure of your eternal destination?" Have you found **"the Way"**? The Son of God, the Lord Jesus Christ, in the evening before His death at Calvary, told His disciples in an upper room in Jerusalem, **"I am *the Way*, the Truth and the Life: no man cometh unto the Father but by Me"** *(John 14.6)*. He is the only Way to God and to God's heaven. Only those who have trusted Him and committed their lives to Him as Lord and Saviour are on the way to heaven. Since nothing that defiles shall ever enter heaven *(Rev. 21.27)*, if we are to be there, it is necessary that, in the words of that chorus, *"our sins are all taken away"*. The Lord Jesus came from heaven to earth with the specific purpose of dying on the cross, the Sinless one for us sinners, to take away our sins and to redeem us from all iniquity. Only by repenting of sin, believing that He died for us, and receiving Him as Saviour from sin and Lord of our lives can we be sure of going to heaven. *"Whosoever believeth in Him shall receive remission of sins"* *(Acts 10.43)*.

This assurance applies to every genuine "born again" believer in Christ, of whatever 'church' or religious affiliation. Every true believer is a part of the church of the living Christ, a member of His Body, part of His Bride, a living stone in His Temple, a sheep in His Flock. Not one will be left behind when He returns to receive His own to Himself *(John 14.3)*. All the family of God – including those with whose practices we may disagree – will be together in universal and eternal harmony with the Lord and with one another!

**"Where are we going?"** The question we are considering is not, however, concerning the believers' eternal future – which is bright and sure – but with the future of the "brethren" assemblies of God's people, the principles we stand for, and our testimony on earth until the Lord comes. There is a story of a little boy who came to his mother one day with a worried look on his face. "Mom", he asked, "that vase on the piano in the living room – has it been handed down from generation to generation?" "Yes", replied his mother, and was about to explain, when her son interrupted, "Well, Mom, this generation has dropped it!"

We have a very beautiful and exceedingly precious treasure: our "assembly heritage". It has been handed down through many generations. These early brethren, in the first half of the 19th century, found it in the word of God, where it had been for many centuries. They passed it on – just as Paul handed on to Timothy *"the things thou hast heard of me among many witnesses"* and instructed him to *"commit"* these truths *"to faithful men, who shall be able to teach others also"*: four generations in one verse *(2 Tim. 2.2)*. Alas, what happened to that vase the little boy dropped has happened to our precious heritage: this generation has dropped it!

This is not the first time this kind of thing has happened! Indeed, it has almost become a pattern with God's people. God delivered His people, Israel, from the bondage of Egypt and gave them a wonderful inheritance, *"a land flowing with milk and honey" (Ex.3.8;* etc.). He warned them to *"walk in My statutes and keep My commandments" (Lev.26.3*, etc.), and not to bow down to, nor serve the gods of the nations in whose lands they were going to dwell *(Ex.23.24,* etc.), or they would lose their land, the heritage God gave them, to their enemies. The book of Joshua records their entry into their inheritance. The very next Bible book, Judges, records how they "dropped it" – repeatedly, in spite of God's mercy in answering their pleas for help and delivering them from their enemies *(Jud. 2.11-23)*.

The days of king David, *"a man after God's own heart" (Acts 13.22)*, were times of great blessing and prosperity for Israel. Neither David nor his people were perfect, but he maintained his love for the Lord and remained true to Him and did not go after the gods of the nations round about. His son, Solomon, however, in spite of being endowed by God with great wisdom, dropped it! He *"went after"* the gods and goddesses of the nations – Ashtoreth, Milcom, Chemosh, Molech, etc.; he *"loved many strange women"* of ungodly nations; *"his heart was turned from the Lord God of Israel" (1 Kings 11.1-9)*. After he died, the kingdom, under his son, Rehoboam, was divided into 2: the Northern kingdom (Israel, also called 'Ephraim') which was consistently evil, with no good kings, and the Southern kingdom (Judah), which had a number of good kings, especially Hezekiah and Josiah, who tried to bring the people back to God; but others, for example, Manasseh, who "dropped it". Eventually, both Israel – in 722 B.C. – and Judah – in 586 B.C. – were taken into captivity by the Assyrians and Babylonians respectively. How sad and serious it was for them to "drop" their precious God-given heritage!

What solemn lessons history has to teach us in our day!

Each of us can truthfully say, with David, *"The lines are fallen unto me in pleasant places; yea, I have a goodly heritage"* *(Ps.16.6)*. We can never lose our inheritance in Christ – it is *"incorruptible, undefiled, and fadeth not away,"* and is *"reserved in heaven"* for us (1 Pet.1.4). But the heritage of truth – of assembly principles – that has been passed on to us can be "dropped" and is being dropped by many who call themselves *"assemblies of God's people"*. Practices held dear by many because they found them in the Scriptures are now being replaced by humanly devised practices that have no place in God's word.

Some assemblies, who, in general, desire to follow the word of God, are, like the Pharisees of old, bound by certain traditions which are not based on Scripture *(Matt. 15.2,3,6)*. One of these is the restriction of reception to those in a similar group of assemblies, thus refusing to welcome godly believers who *'follow not with us"*. The Lord's response to His disciples who acted in this way is appropriate for us: *"Forbid him not: for he that is not against us is for us" (Luke 9.50)*. One of the dearly held principles of the early "brethren" was the reception of all believers, regardless of their religious affiliation, provided they were living godly lives and did not teach false doctrine. For example, Anthony Norris Groves wrote to J.G. Bellett that it came to him as a revelation from heaven that all believers shared the common life of the body of Christ, and that sectarian walls were, therefore, man-made elements dividing Christians who were spiritually bound together in Christ. Life, not light was the measure of communion. J.N. Darby, in the first brethren pamphlet ever published, wrote, *"He is an enemy to the work of the Spirit of God who seeks the interests of any particular denomination... No meeting, which is not framed to embrace all the children of God...can find the fulness of blessing."*[1] Again, J.N. Darby, in a letter in 1839, wrote, *"Whenever Christ has received a person, we should receive him...As our table is the Lord's and not ours, we receive all the Lord has received... You say, 'Would you receive a Roman Catholic?' If a Roman Catholic really extolled Jesus as Saviour, owned*

*His one sacrifice of Himself as the sole putting away of sin, he would cease to be a Roman Catholic in the evil sense of the word, and on these terms only would he be with us.*"[2] Wm. Kelly shared the same view, expressed in a letter written in 1875, *"Scripture knows nothing of keeping outside a godly-walking member of Christ."*[3] To refuse to welcome to our fellowship believers who are living godly lives, is thus *"dropping"* part of the heritage that has been left to us, not only in the Scriptures, but by early "brethren" leaders.

However, consideration of preserving our heritage leads us to think of many aspects of that heritage that are being "dropped" in many assemblies today, and which we should seek to preserve because they are Scriptural principles. They include:

*1. **Appointment of one man as the pastor or minister of each church.*** Dr. Edward Cronin might be said to be "the founder" of the "brethren movement" in Dublin. One of the main reasons he had for leaving organized churches was his growing repugnance to "one-man ministry" – a practice which he could not find in the Scriptures.[4] In recent years, many assemblies are returning to the situation that these early "brethren" left in order to follow Scriptural precepts and pattern. There is a parallel to this in the history of God's earthly people. In the days of Samuel, God's appointed prophet and judge, they demanded that he make them a king to judge them *"**like all the nations**" (1 Sam.8.5)*. *"The thing displeased Samuel"*, but God assured him that they were not rejecting Samuel but the Lord Himself. So it is today: God's purpose and design are expressed clearly in His word, but His word is set aside in favour of man's word and man's desire to be "like all the 'churches'". "One-man ministry" denies three important principles which have been considered in these studies:

*a.* **Plurality of Elders in every church.** To those who assert that the "pastor" is the "teaching elder", it should be pointed out that all elders should be **"apt to teach"** *(1 Tim.3.2)*. Not all may have the spiritual gift of teaching; not all may be able to teach from the pulpit, but all should be teachers, able to ' *feed the church of God" (Acts 20.28).*

*b.* **Diversity and Multiplicity of Spiritual Gifts,** which should be developed and encouraged in each local church. These gifts include the gift of teaching. If "the pastor" is doing all or most of the teaching and preaching (including evangelism) the development of teaching gift is hindered. It is noteworthy that Paul, apostle though he was, is not recorded as having remained for more than three years in any local church. While in Ephesus for 2-3 years, he wrote *1 Corinthians,* giving instruction on gifts and their use in the church *(chapters 12-14).* He would have been most hypocritical to write these chapters had he not encouraged the development of gift in Ephesus. The elders he called to Miletus a year later must have been "apt to teach": he had taught and trained them!

*c.* **The Priesthood of every believer** as indicated in *1 Pet. 2.5,9.* Since all believers are constituted *"an holy priesthood",* there should be opportunity within each assembly for them to *"offer up spiritual sacrifices",* such as praise *(Heb.13.15)* – not just for one person to lead in worship. As a *"royal priesthood",* they should have the privilege of *"showing forth the praises"* (excellencies, glories) of the Lord Who has called them.

In addition, it is an increasingly demanded requirement of "pastors" to have Seminary training. Now, theological training is very valuable, but it should not be a prerequisite to teaching in the local assembly. It certainly was not in the early church! The religious leaders marvelled at the apostles, Peter and John, because they realized they were *"unlearned and ignorant men"* – not formally trained in the rabbinical schools –– yet able to speak with remarkable clarity and authority from the Scriptures. They recognized *"that they had been with Jesus" (Acts 4.13).* It is very possible to have seminary training without spiritual qualifications! Today, many formerly fundamental, evangelical colleges deny some of the foundations of the faith – even the inerrancy of Scripture; and very few accept and teach New Testament church principles.

Usually, "pastors" appointed to this ministry are given a stated salary. Even Paul did not have this (see *Phil. 4.10-19*) and there is no instruction in the N.T. about fixed salaries for Christian workers, although the need to support missionaries, evangelists and teachers is clearly stated *(Phil. 4.10-19; 1 Cor. 9.1-14; Gal. 6.6)*.

*2. Public participation of sisters in meetings of the church,* in prayer, teaching, speaking at the Lord's Supper, etc. Closely related to this is:

*3. Abandonment of head covering in church gatherings* – which is frequently a prelude to the introduction of women's participation.

*4. De-emphasis on the Lord's Supper*, sometimes reducing its frequency and the time allotted for it.

*5. Reduced emphasis on evangelism,* with watering down of the Gospel message in relation to sin, judgment, repentance; and replacement of preaching by entertainment.

*6. Charismatic infiltration* in some assemblies.

*PRESERVING OUR HERITAGE.* **What to do about it?** These are some of the problems that are making inroads into assemblies, at least in many parts of North America. How can we stem the tide? What principles should influence our thinking and our actions?

*1.* **Give Priority to the Word of God.** Adhere to the truths and principles of Scripture at all costs! In his last recorded writing, Paul warned Timothy that things would deteriorate in the world, and that **"perilous times shall come"**. They are already here! The description he gives in **2 Tim. 3 and 4** is up-to-date. **"Evil men and seducers"** are already waxing **"worse and worse deceiving and being deceived"** (**3.13**). People in our society are already turning **"away their ears from the truth and...are turned to fables"** (**4.4**). What is the safeguard for believers, the antidote to this trouble? In the centre of the passage (**3.14-17**), Paul urges his younger friend and colleague to **"continue...in the things which thou hast learned.. knowing ...that from a child thou hast known the Holy Scriptures which are able to make thee wise unto salvation through faith...in Christ Jesus"**. All Scripture is God-breathed, through human channels, chosen by God, and **"is profitable for doctrine,"** – to teach what is right – **"for reproof,"** – to show what is not right – **"for correction,"** – to set right – **"for instruction in righteousness"** – to train in what is right. In his introduction to T. S. *Veitch's "Story of the Brethren Movement", George Goodman* wrote, *"The troubles that arise among the churches of the saints come never from obedience to the Truth, always from departure from it."*[5]

**Dangers of Departing from Scriptural teaching.** God has given us a route plan for each believer individually and for each church: the directions are contained in His word. Many are setting aside this Guide-book, feeling that their own plan, or the route others are taking may be more attractive and effective in our modern culture (different from the Corinthian or Ephesian culture!). Just as in a drive or a walk, departure from the planned route can take us far from the desired destination and land us in serious problems, so deviation from God's instructions contained in His word can lead us further and further from His route, His blessing – and from Himself. For example, discarding of head-covering by sisters in the Family Bible Hour or prayer meeting leads, in a short time, to sisters coming uncovered to the Lord's Supper. The next step in this wrong path is audible participation by sisters in the prayer-meeting, followed by the Lord's Supper. Later, they are teaching in the regular church meetings, and are recognized as elders. This is not a hypothetical scenario but one which has actually taken place in different assemblies! In many denominational churches, all around us, the departure from the word of God has proceeded further. They began by discarding N.T. church principles, believing them not to be important. With the passage of a few years, the inerrancy of Scripture has been jettisoned (this, even by some in assemblies), followed by denial of the truth of the record of creation and the flood; then the deity of Christ, His virgin birth, atoning death and bodily resurrection. Of course, the decline does not end there – though that itself is tragic in the extreme. Now, in many "Christian churches", there has come a serious breakdown of moral standards: immorality and such practices as homosexuality are permitted, even in "ministers"! What began as an apparently pleasant side-path in our route has become a disastrous slippery slope that has led to destruction and ruin! Could this happen in assemblies? I trust not! But don't be too sure! It is very serious to defy the word of God! It is vital to adhere to it at any price!

*2.* **Differentiate between divine principles and Scriptural practices on the one hand and human traditions on the other.** Human traditions can be good, bad or indifferent! Any tradition based on the unerring word of God can only be good and should obviously be continued. Other traditions – beliefs and practices handed down from one church to another or from one generation to another – may have outlived their usefulness. For example, the time for church meetings need not be the same for 100 years! Nor is it necessary to maintain the same format of meetings, arrangements of speakers or the type of building. Practices based on convenience, apparent benefit at the time, or simply on habit and custom, without any Scriptural endorsement, should not be tenaciously retained as if they were in the category of divine commands and had the authority of the word of God.

*3.* **Maintain "love to all saints" (Eph. 1.15; Col. 1.4; Phmn. 5)**, including those who take opposing views on church principles and practices! Remember one of the last commands of our beloved Lord, before He went to Calvary, recorded five times in His last discourse to His disciples on the eve of Calvary: **"Love one another" (John 13.34 – twice, 35; 15.12,17).** This is probably the most frequent command in the New Testament, being repeated ten times in the epistles, as well as many times in other forms. It might be considered the most important responsibility that each of us has to our local assembly, and indeed to all the church. Many of the "one another" commands of the New Testament have love as their basis, for example, *"By love serve one another" (Gal. 5.13);* *"Forbearing one another in love" (Eph. 4.2)*; *"Be ye kind one to another, tenderhearted, forgiving one another" (Eph. 4.32); "Consider one another to provoke unto love" (Heb. 10.24); "Having compassion one of another in love, love as brethren" (1 Pet. 3.8)*, etc. and, negatively, *"Speak not evil one of another" (James 4.11); "Grudge not one against another" (James 5.9);* etc.

**CONCLUSION. "Preserving our heritage"** should be a priority in the life of every believer in every assembly of God's people, not sacrificing N.T. principles, but tenaciously holding to divine truth and graciously manifesting divine love.

In the days of Ahab, the wicked king of Israel, and his equally, or even more, wicked wife, Jezebel, a close neighbour of Ahab, Naboth the Jezreelite, had a vineyard *"hard by the palace of Ahab king of Samaria" (1 Kings 21.1)* Ahab eyed it with envy and asked Naboth to give it to him, offering him "a better vineyard", or "the worth of it in money" in return. Naboth's response is worth noting: **"The Lord forbid that I should give the inheritance of my fathers unto thee"** *(v.3)*. Naboth was convinced that this portion of land was not really his to barter away, even for more than it was worth. It was the Lord's land. It was the inheritance given by the Lord to his fathers and handed down from generation to generation. It was a heritage from the Lord – and Naboth was not prepared to drop it, even for the king of Israel!

In the pages of God's word, we have a very precious heritage handed down to us from generation to generation. Satan would have us give it up. He offers all kinds of benefits to us in exchange for God's heritage. Let us not drop it! Let us say with Naboth, **"God forbid that I should give the inheritance of my fathers unto thee."**

1. Beattie, D.J.: "Brethren: The Story of a Great Recovery" (John Ritchie Ltd., Kilmarnock, 1940), p.14.

2. Ironside, H.A.: "A Historical Sketch of the Brethren Movement" (Loizeaux Brothers, Neptune, N.J., Revised, 1985), pp.34,35.
3. Ibid, p.97.
4. Ibid, p.11.
5. Veitch, T.S.: "The Story of the Brethren Movement": 'Introduction' by George Goodman.